BARCELONA

ANNELISE SORENSEN
& RYAN CHANDLER

DK | Penguin Random House

Top 10 Barcelona Highlights

The Top 10 of Everything

CONTENTS

Barcelona Area by Area

Streetsmart

Within each Top 10 list in this book, no hierarchy of quality or popularity is implied. All 10 are, in the editor's opinion, of roughly equal merit.

Front cover and spine *The astonishing Sagrada Família viewed from Plaça de Gaudí*
Back cover *Plaça Reial in the Barri Gòtic*
Title page *Nativity façade of the Sagrada Família*

Welcome to
Barcelona

On the shores of the Mediterranean, the Catalan capital boasts one of Europe's largest, best-preserved medieval quarters and the finest collection of *Modernista* architecture anywhere. It also has exciting contemporary design, world-renowned cuisine and a buzzing nightlife. With Eyewitness Top 10 Barcelona, it's yours to explore.

For all its apparent big-city bustle, Barcelona is a place to linger, whether on the palm-shaded seafront, over coffee in a medieval square or picnicking at **Parc Güell** or in a **Montjuïc** garden. The best way to experience the city is on foot, getting lost in the stone labyrinth of **Barri Gòtic** or taking time to notice the details – ceramic garlands, wrought-iron balustrades, vibrant tiles – on the **Eixample** *Modernista* mansions. The streets are full of **public art**, from Haring murals to Lichtenstein sculptures, and there are a host of fantastic **museums** dedicated to Picasso, Miró, contemporary art and more.

Modern Catalan cuisine is innovative and daring, and alongside molecular gastronomy in award-winning restaurants, you'll find places serving fabulous local produce the way they've done for generations. At the colourful local festivals you'll get an insight into what makes Barcelona so different from the rest of Spain. No flamenco here – instead you can admire the locals as they build towering *castells* or dodge fire-spitting demons and dragons in the *correfocs*.

Whether you're coming for a weekend or a week, our Top 10 guide describes the best of everything that Barcelona has to offer, from Gaudí's greatest masterpiece, the **Sagrada Família**, to the 18th-century maze in **Parc del Laberint d'Horta**. There are tips throughout, from seeking out what's free to avoiding the crowds, plus nine easy-to-follow itineraries, designed to tie together a clutch of sights in a short space of time. Add inspiring photography and detailed maps, and you've got the essential pocket-sized travel companion. **Enjoy the book, and enjoy Barcelona**.

Clockwise from top: **Museu Nacional d'Art de Catalunya**; stained-glass dome at the Palau de la Música Catalana; La Pedrera's chimneys; Parc Güell; Casa Batlló's windows; maze at the Parc del Laberint d'Horta; Museu d'Art Contemporani and Centre de Cultura Contemporània

Exploring Barcelona

You'll be utterly spoiled for choice for things to see and do in Barcelona, which is packed with historical buildings, parks, museums and beaches. Whether you're coming for a weekend, or want to get to know the city better, these two- and four-day itineraries will help you make the most of your visit.

Two Days in Barcelona

Day ❶
MORNING
Stroll along Barcelona's most celebrated avenue, **La Rambla** *(see pp16–17)*, then dive into the warren of medieval streets that makes up the Barri Gòtic and visit **Barcelona Cathedral** *(see pp18–19)*.

AFTERNOON
Continue your exploration of Barcelona's historic heart with a wander around the Born neighbourhood. Visit the **Museu Picasso** *(see pp30–31)*, then see if you can get tickets for an evening performance at the lavish *Modernista* **Palau de la Música Catalana** *(see pp32–3)*.

Day ❷
MORNING
Spend the morning marvelling at Gaudí's incredible **Sagrada Família** *(see pp12–15)*, but make sure you've booked tickets online in advance to avoid the long queues.

AFTERNOON
Ride the funicular up the green hill of Montjuïc to the **Fundació Joan Miró** *(see pp28–9)*, a stunning modern building that is home to a spectacular collection of Miró's work.

Four Days in Barcelona

Day ❶
MORNING
Make the day's first stop the playful, whimsical **Parc Güell** *(see pp22–3)*, a UNESCO World Heritage Site.

AFTERNOON
Head south to the city's most iconic building, the **Sagrada Família** *(see pp12–15)*, then take in the **Museu**

The vibrant Mercat de la Boqueria is one of Europe's largest markets for fresh produce, cheese and meat.

Font Màgica

Museu Nacional d'Art de Catalunya

Jardins Laribel

MONTJUÏC

Fundació Joan Miró

Parc de Montjuïc funicular station

FUNICUL

Jardins de Miramar

Picasso *(see pp30–31)*, set in a complex of five interconnected Gothic palaces. Book tickets online in advance to avoid queues at these attractions.

Day ❷
MORNING
Take a stroll along **La Rambla** *(see pp16–17)*, perhaps ducking into the **Mercat de la Boqueria** *(see p68)* to admire the dizzying range of produce. Then meander through the medieval lanes of the Barri Gòtic to find **Barcelona Cathedral** *(see pp18–19)*.

AFTERNOON
Take in the smart boutiques of the elegant **Passeig de Gràcia** *(see p66)*, then visit one of Gaudí's most remarkable buildings, **La Pedrera** *(see pp26–7)*. In summer, you can stick around for jazz on its famous undulating rooftop.

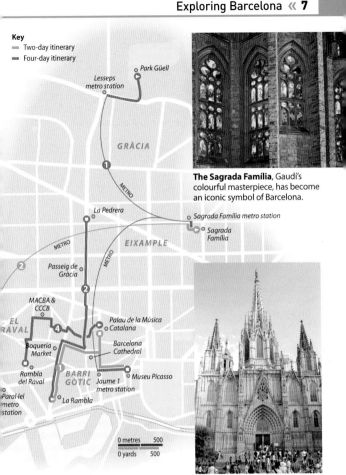

Key
— Two-day itinerary
— Four-day itinerary

Park Güell

Lesseps metro station

METRO

GRÀCIA

The Sagrada Família, Gaudí's colourful masterpiece, has become an iconic symbol of Barcelona.

La Pedrera

Sagrada Família metro station

Sagrada Família

METRO

EIXAMPLE

Passeig de Gràcia

METRO

MACBA & CCCB

Palau de la Música Catalana

Boqueria Market

Barcelona Cathedral

Rambla del Raval

BARRI GÒTIC

Jaume 1 metro station

Museu Picasso

Paral·lel metro station

La Rambla

0 metres 500
0 yards 500

Barcelona's 13th-century cathedral has a magnificent façade and a quiet cloister.

Day ❸
MORNING
Relax in one of the many gardens on Montjuïc, perhaps the charming **Jardins Laribel** or the leafy groves of **Jardins de Miramar** *(see p98)*, before visiting the **Fundació Joan Miró** *(see pp28–9)*, one of the world's largest Miró collections.
AFTERNOON
You'd need more than an afternoon to see every gallery at the **Museu Nacional d'Art de Catalunya** *(see pp20–21)*, but the Romanesque and Gothic collections are a must. In the evening, enjoy the sound and light show at the **Font Màgica** *(see p95)*.

Day ❹
MORNING
Take a tour of the **Palau de la Música Catalana** *(see pp32–3)*, a breathtaking *Modernista* masterpiece with an eye-popping auditorium.
AFTERNOON
Check out the contemporary art at the **Museu d'Art Contemporani (MACBA)** and **Centre de Cultura Contemporània (CCCB)** *(see pp34–5)*, then relax over a coffee on the nearby **Rambla del Raval** *(see p88)*.

Top 10 Barcelona Highlights

The soaring, tree-like columns
of the Sagrada Família's nave

🔟 Barcelona Highlights

Blessed with desirable geographical genes, this sparkling Mediterranean jewel has it all, from beautiful *Modernista* buildings, atmospheric medieval streets and enchanting squares to beaches, treasure-filled museums and a thriving port area.

Sagrada Família ①
Gaudí's otherworldly *pièce de résistance* is the enduring symbol of the city and its *Modernista* legacy. Eight of the 18 planned spires jut into the sky *(see pp12–15)*.

② La Rambla
Barcelona's centrepiece, this thriving pedestrian thoroughfare cuts a wide swathe through the old town, from Plaça de Catalunya to the glittering Mediterranean Sea *(see pp16–17)*.

③ Barcelona Cathedral
Dominating the heart of the old town is this magnificent Gothic cathedral, with a soaring, elaborate façade and a graceful, sun-dappled cloister containing palm trees and white geese *(see pp18–19)*.

AVINGUDA GRAN VIA DE LE
AVINGUDA DEL PARAL·LEL
RONDA DE SANT PAU
EL RAVAL
MONTJUÏC
Parc de Montjuïc
④ ⑦ ⑩

Museu Nacional d'Art de Catalunya ④
The stately Palau Nacional is home to the Museu Nacional d'Art de Catalunya (MNAC). Its extensive collections boast some of the world's finest Romanesque art, rescued from churches around Catalonia during the 1920s *(see pp20–21)*.

⑤ Parc Güell
With its whimsical dragon, fairy-tale pavilions and sinuous bench offering dramatic city views, this magical hillside park is indubitably the work of Gaudí *(see pp22–3)*.

6 La Pedrera

Unmistakably Gaudí, this *Modernista* marvel seems to grow from the very pavement itself. Its curving façade is fluid and alive, and mosaic chimneys keep watch over the rooftop like shrewd-eyed knights *(see pp26–7)*.

7 Fundació Joan Miró

An incomparable blend of art and architecture, this museum showcases the work of Joan Miró, one of Catalonia's greatest 20th-century artists. Paintings, sculptures, drawings and textiles represent 60 prolific years *(see pp28–9)*.

8 Museu Picasso

Housed in a medieval palace complex, this museum charts Picasso's rise to fame with an extensive collection of his early works, including numerous masterful portraits that he painted at the age of 13 *(see pp30–31)*.

0 metres	500
0 yards	500

Parc de la Ciutadella

9 Palau de la Música Catalana

No mere concert hall, the aptly-named Palace of Catalan Music is one of the finest, and most exemplary, *Modernista* buildings in Barcelona *(see pp32–3)*.

10 Museu d'Art Contemporani and Centre de Cultura Contemporània

The city's gleaming contemporary art museum and its cutting-edge cultural centre have sparked an urban revival in the El Raval area *(see pp34–5)*.

🔟 ⭐ Sagrada Família

Nothing prepares you for the impact of the Sagrada Família. A *tour de force* of the imagination, Antoni Gaudí's church has provoked endless controversy. It also offers visitors the unique chance to watch a wonder of the world in the making. Over the last 90 years, at incalculable cost, sculptors and architects have continued to build Gaudí's dream. Now financed by over a million visitors each year, it is hoped the project will be complete by 2026, the 100th anniversary of Gaudí's death.

4 Nativity Façade
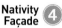
Gaudí's love of nature is visible in this façade **(right)**. Up to 100 plant and animal species are sculpted in stone, and the two main columns are supported by turtles.

1 Spiral Staircases

These helicoidal stone stairways **(above)**, which wind up the bell towers, look like snail shells.

2 Hanging Model
This contraption is testimony to Gaudí's ingenuity. He made the 3D device – using chains and tiny weighted sacks of lead pellets – as a model for the arches and vaulted ceilings of the Colònia Güell crypt. No one in the history of architecture had ever designed a building like this.

5 Passion Façade
Created between 1954 and 2002, this Josep Subirachs façade represents the sacrifice and pain of Jesus. The difference between the Gothic feel of Subirachs' style and the intricacy of Gaudí's work has been controversial.

6 Spires
For a close-up look at the mosaic tiling and gargoyles on the spires **(right)**, take the lift up inside the bell tower for views that are equally spectacular.

3 Nave
The immense central body of the church **(right)**, now complete, is made up of leaning, tree-like columns with branches that are inspired by a banana tree spreading out across the ceiling; the overall effect is that of a beautiful stone forest.

Sagrada Família Floorplan

7 Rosario's Claustro

In the only cloister to be finished by Gaudí, the imagery is thought to be inspired by the anarchist riots that began in 1909 (see pp38–9). The Devil's temptation of man is represented by the sculpture of a serpent wound around a rebel.

8 Apse

Adorned with lizards, serpents and four gigantic snails, the apse was the first section of the church to be completed by Gaudí.

9 Crypt Museum

Gaudí now lies in the crypt (right), and his tomb is visible from the museum. Using audio-visual exhibits, the museum provides information about the construction of the church. The highlight is the maquette workshop, producing scale models for the ongoing work.

10 Unfinished Business

The church buzzes with activity: sculptors dangle from spires, stonemasons carve huge slabs of stone and cranes and scaffolding litter the site. Observing the construction in progress allows visitors to grasp the monumental scale of the project.

NEED TO KNOW

MAP G2 ■ Entrances: C/Marina (for groups) and C/Sardenya ■ 93 207 30 31 ■ www.sagradafamilia.org

Open 9am–6pm daily (to 7pm Mar & Oct, 8pm Apr–Sep)

Adm €15 (€22 with audio guide); €24 for combined ticket with Casa-Museu Gaudí, including audio guide; €29 including lift access to the towers. Advance online booking is recommended.

For full details of guided tours visit the website.

■ Sit in a terrace bar on nearby Av Gaudí and drink in the view of Gaudí's masterpiece illuminated at night.

■ For the best photos, get here before 8am: the light on the Nativity Façade is excellent and the tour buses haven't yet arrived.

■ In the cryptogram on the Passion Façade, the numbers add up to the age of Christ at his death.

Sight Guide
The main entrance is on C/Marina, in front of the Nativity Façade, along with gift shops. There is a lift in each façade (stairs are not open to the public). The museum is near the entrance on C/Sardenya. Eight of the 18 planned towers are built and are open to the public, but these are not accessible for those with disabilities.

Key Sagrada Família Dates

 1882
The first stone of the Sagrada Família is officially laid, with architect Francesc del Villar heading the project. Villar soon resigns after disagreements with the church's religious founders.

2 1883
The young, up-and-coming Antoni Gaudí is commissioned as the principal architect. He goes on to devote the next 40 years of his life to the project: by the end he even lives on the premises.

3 1889
The church crypt is completed, ringed by a series of chapels, one of which is later to house Gaudí's tomb.

Sculpture, Passion Façade

4 1904
The final touches are made to the Nativity Façade, which depicts Jesus, Mary and Joseph amid a chorus of angels.

5 1925
The first of the 18 planned bell towers, measuring 100 m (328 ft) in height, is finished.

6 1926
On 10 June, Gaudí is killed by a tram while crossing the street near his beloved church. No one recognizes the city's most famous architect.

7 1936
The military uprising and the advent of the Spanish Civil War brings construction of the Sagrada Família to a halt for some 20 years. During this period, Gaudí's studio and the crypt in the Sagrada Família are burned by revolutionaries, who despise the Catholic church for siding with the nationalists.

8 1987–1990
Sculptor and painter Josep Maria Subirachs (b.1927) takes to living in the Sagrada Família just as his famous predecessor did. Subirachs completes the statuary of the Passion Façade. His angular, severe and striking sculptures draw both criticism and praise.

9 2000
On 31 December, the nave is at long last declared complete.

10 2010–2026
The interior of the church is completed, and in November 2010 Pope Benedict XVI consecrated it as a basilica. The completion of the entire Sagrada Família is forecast for 2026. The building of the Sagrada Família – as Gaudí intended – relies on donations. With so many paying visitors pouring in daily, construction work is gaining momentum.

Stained-glass windows in the apse

ANTONI GAUDÍ

Gaudí (1852–1926)

A flag bearer for the *Modernista* movement of the late 19th century, Antoni Gaudí is Barcelona's most famous architect. A strong Catalan nationalist and a devout Catholic, he led an almost monastic life, consumed by his architectural vision and living in virtual poverty for most of his life. In 2003 the Vatican opened the beatification process for Gaudí, which is the first step towards declaring his sainthood. Gaudí's extraordinary legacy dominates the architectural map of Barcelona. His name itself comes from the Catalan verb *gaudir*, meaning "to enjoy", and an enormous sense of exuberance and playfulness pervades his work. As was characteristic of *Modernisme*, nature prevails, not only in the decorative motifs, but also in the very structure of Gaudí's buildings. His highly innovative style is also characterized by intricate wrought-iron gates and balconies and *trencadís* tiling.

TOP 10
GAUDÍ SIGHTS IN BARCELONA

1 **Sagrada Família**
2 **La Pedrera** (1910)
see pp26–7
3 **Parc Güell** (1900)
see pp22–3
4 **Casa Batlló** (1905)
see p45
5 **Palau Güell** (1890)
see p87
6 **Torre Bellesguard** (1875)
7 **Finca Güell** (1887)
8 **Casa Calvet** (1899)
9 **Colegio Teresiano** (1890)
10 **Casa Vicens** (1885)

Casa Batlló's many chimneys are adorned with tiled designs. These usually unremarkable parts of a building have become Gaudí's whimsical trademark.

TOP 10 ⭐ La Rambla

There may be no better place in the country to indulge in the Spanish ritual of the *paseo* (stroll) than on this wide pedestrian street. Despite a terrorist attack in August 2017, La Rambla remains a lively hub of exuberant activity. Human statues stand motionless among the passers-by; buskers croon crowd-pleasing classics; caricaturists deftly sketch faces; bustling stalls sell bright bouquets and souvenirs; and round-the-clock kiosks sell everything from *The Financial Times* to adult videos.

Gran Teatre del Liceu ①

The city's grand opera house **(right)**, founded in 1847, brought Catalan opera stars such as Montserrat Caballé to the world. Twice gutted by fire, it has been fully restored *(see p54)*.

Crowds on La Rambla

② Mercat de la Boqueria

A cacophonous shrine to food, this cavernous market has it all, from stacks of fruit to suckling pigs and fresh lobsters *(see p68)*.

③ Flower Stalls

La Rambla is teeming with life and things to distract the eye, but the true Rambla old-timers are the flower stalls flanking the pedestrian walkway, many run by the same families for decades.

④ Monument a Colom

Pointing resolutely out to sea, this 1888 bronze statue of Christopher Columbus **(left)** commemorates his return to Spain after discovering the Americas. An elevator whisks visitors to the top of the column for sensational views *(see p102)*.

Font de Canaletes ⑤

Ensure that you come back to the city by sipping water from this 19th-century fountain **(right)**, inscribed with the legend that those who drink from it "will fall in love with Barcelona and always return".

6 Miró Mosaic

Splashed on the walkway on La Rambla is a colourful pavement mosaic by Catalan artist Joan Miró. His signature abstract shapes and primary colours unfold at your feet *(see p71)*.

7 Palau de la Virreina

This Neo-Classical palace was built by the viceroy of Peru in 1778. Today, the Palace of the Viceroy's Wife is home to the Culture Institute, run by the city council, and hosts art exhibitions and cultural events.

La Rambla

8 Bruno Quadras Building

Once an umbrella factory, this playful, late 19th-century building **(above)** is festooned with umbrellas.

9 Arts Santa Mònica

Once the hallowed haunt of rosary beads and murmured prayers, this former 17th-century monastery was reborn in the 1980s – thanks to a massive government-funded facelift – as a cutting-edge contemporary art centre. Exhibitions range from sculpture to large-scale video installations and photography.

10 Església de Betlem

A relic from a time when the Catholic Church was rolling in pesetas (and power), this hulking 17th-century church is a seminal reminder of when La Rambla was more religious than risqué *(see p41)*.

NEED TO KNOW

Mercat de La Boqueria: **MAP L3**; La Rambla 91; 8am–8:30pm Mon–Sat; www.boqueria.info

Palau de la Virreina: **MAP L3**; La Rambla 99; noon–8pm Tue–Sun; Cultural Information Centre 10am–8:30pm daily; ajuntament.barcelona.cat/lavirreina/en

Gran Teatre del Liceu: **MAP L4**; La Rambla 51–59; www.liceubarcelona.cat

Arts Santa Mònica: **MAP L5**; La Rambla 7; 11am–9pm Tue–Sat, 11am–5pm Sun; www.artssantamonica.cat

■ Kick back at the Cafè de l'Òpera at No. 74 *(see p64)* and soak up the Rambla ambience with a cool *granissat* (crushed ice drink) in hand.

■ La Rambla is rife with pickpockets – be careful with your belongings.

🔟 ⭐ Barcelona Cathedral

From its Gothic cloister and Baroque chapels to its splendid 19th-century façade, the cathedral, dating from 1298, is an amalgam of architectural styles, each one paying homage to a period in Spain's religious history. Records show that an early Christian baptistry was established here in the 6th century, later replaced by a Romanesque basilica in the 11th century, which gave way to the current Gothic cathedral. This living monument still functions as the Barri Gòtic's spiritual hub.

① Main Façade
The 19th-century façade **(below)** has the entrance, flanked by twin towers, *Modernista* stained-glass windows and 100 carved angels. The restoration process took 8 years and was completed in 2011.

② Choirstalls
The lavish choir-stalls (1340), crowned with wooden spires, are decorated with colourful coats of arms by artist Joan de Borgonya.

④ Nave and Organ
The immense nave **(above)** is supported by soaring Gothic buttresses, which arch over 16 chapels. The 16th-century organ looming over the interior fills the space with music during services.

③ Cloister
Graced with a fountain, palm trees and roaming geese, the cloister dates back to the 14th century. The mossy fountain is presided over by a small iron statue of Sant Jordi – St George (see p41).

Crypt of Santa Eulàlia ⑤
In the centre of the crypt lies the graceful 1327 alabaster sarcophagus **(right)** of Santa Eulàlia, Barcelona's first patron saint. Reliefs depict her martyrdom.

6 Capella de Sant Benet
Honouring Sant Benet, the patron saint of Europe, this chapel showcases the 15th-century altarpiece *Transfiguration of the Lord* by illustrious Catalan artist Bernat Martorell.

7 Capella de Santa Llúcia
This lovely Romanesque chapel is dedicated to Santa Llúcia, the patron saint of eyes and vision *(see p41)*. On her saint's day (13 December), the blind come to pray at her chapel.

**Cathedral
Floorplan**

8 Capella del Santíssim Sacrament i Crist de Lepant
This 15th-century chapel features the Crist de Lepant **(right)** which, legend has it, guided the Christian fleet in its 16th-century battle against the Ottoman Turks.

9 Pia Almoina and Gaudí Exhibition Centre
The 11th-century Pia Almoina, once a rest house for pilgrims and the poor, houses the Gaudí Exhibition Centre where a collection of objects by Antoni Gaudí can be found.

10 Casa de l'Ardiaca
Originally built in the 12th century, the Archdeacon's House is located near what was once the Bishop's Gate in the city's Roman walls. Expanded over the centuries, it now includes a lovely leafy patio with a fountain.

NEED TO KNOW

Cathedral: MAP M3 ■ Pl de la Seu ■ 93 342 82 62 ■ www.catedralbcn.org ■ 8am–7.30pm Mon–Fri, to 8pm Sat & Sun ■ Free for cathedral floor and cloister (€7 donation 1–5pm Mon–Sat, 2–5pm Sun); choir and rooftops (via lift) €3 each; guided tours 11am–1pm Mon–Sat by reservation, tel: 93 315 22 13

Casa de l'Ardiaca: MAP M3 ■ C/Santa Llúcia 1

■ 9am–8:45pm Mon–Fri (to 1pm Sun); Jul–Aug: 9am–7:30pm Mon–Fri

Gaudí Exhibition Centre: MAP N3 ■ Av de la Catedral 4 ■ Apr–Oct: 10am–8pm daily; Nov–Mar: 10am–6pm daily ■ €15

■ **Dress modestly to visit the cathedral** (covered shoulders; no shorts).

■ **Choral/organ concerts** are usually held monthly; enquire at the Pia Almoina.

■ **Watch** *sardanes* – Catalonia's regional dance – in Plaça de la Seu (6pm Sat, noon Sun).

Cathedral Guide
The most impressive entrance is the main portal on Plaça de la Seu. As you enter, to the left lie a series of chapels, the organ and elevators up to the roof. The Gaudí Exhibition Centre is to the left of the main entrance; Casa de l'Ardiaca is to the right.

🔟 ⭐ Museu Nacional d'Art de Catalunya

Holding one of the most important medieval art collections in the world, the Museu Nacional d'Art de Catalunya (MNAC) is housed in the majestic Palau Nacional, built in 1929. The highlight is the Romanesque art section, consisting of the painted interiors of Pyrenean churches dating from the 11th and 12th centuries. Other collections include works by Catalan artists from the early 19th century to the present day.

① The Madonna of the Councillors
Commissioned by the city council in 1443, this work by Lluís Dalmau is rich in political symbolism, with the head councillors, saints and martyrs kneeling before an enthroned Virgin.

② Murals: Santa Maria de Taüll
The well-preserved interior of Santa Maria de Taüll (c.1123) gives an idea of how colourful the Romanesque churches must have been. There are scenes from Jesus's early life, with John the Baptist and the Wise Men.

③ Cambó Bequest
Catalan politician Francesc Cambó (1876–1974) left his huge art collection to Catalonia; two large galleries contain works from the 16th to early 19th centuries, including Tiepolo's 1756 *The Minuet* **(above)**.

④ Thyssen-Bornemisza Collection
A small but fine selection from Baron Thyssen-Bornemisza's vast collection. Among the magnificent paintings are Fra Angelico's sublime *Madonna of Humility* (1433–5) and a charmingly domestic *Madonna and Child* (c.1618) by Rubens **(left)**.

⑤ Frescoes: Sant Climent de Taüll
The interior of Sant Climent de Taüll **(below)** is a melange of French, Byzantine and Italian influences. The apse is dominated by *Christ in Majesty* and the symbols of the four Evangelists and the Virgin, with the apostles beneath.

⑦ Woman with Hat and Fur Collar

Picasso's extraordinary depiction of his lover Maria-Thérèse Walter shows him moving beyond Cubism and Surrealism into a new personal language, soon to be known simply as the "Picasso style".

⑨ Confidant from the Batlló House

Among the fine *Modernista* furnishings are some exquisite pieces by Antoni Gaudí, including an undulating wooden chair designed to encourage confidences between friends.

⑥ Ramon Casas and Pere Romeu on a Tandem

This painting **(above)** depicts the painter Casas and his friend Romeu, with whom he began the bohemian Barri Gòtic tavern Els Quatre Gats.

⑧ Crucifix of Batlló Majesty

This splendid, mid-12th-century wooden carving depicts Christ on the cross with open eyes and no signs of suffering, as he has defeated death.

⑩ Numismatics

The public numismatic collection dates back to the 6th century BC and features medals, coins **(above)** (including those from the Greek colony of Empuries, which had its own mint from the 5th century BC), early paper money and 15th-century Italian bills.

⑩ Numismatics
⑥ Ramon Casas and Pere Romeu on a Tandem
④ Thyssen-Bornemisza Collection
③ Cambó Bequest

⑨ Confidant from the Batlló House
⑦ Woman with Hat and Fur Collar
② Murals: Santa Maria de Taüll
⑤ Frescoes: Sant Climent de Taüll
① The Madonna of the Councillors
⑧ Crucifix of Batlló Majesty

Key to Floorplan

- Romanesque Art Gallery
- Modern Art; Drawings, Prints and Posters
- Gothic Art Gallery
- Renaissance and Baroque Art
- Library

NEED TO KNOW

MAP B4 ▪ Palau Nacional, Parc de Montjuïc ▪ www.museunacional.cat/en

Open 10am–6pm Tue–Sat (to 8pm May–Sep), 10am–3pm Sun; timings for roof terrace vary, check website.

Adm €12, concessions €8.40 (valid for 2 days in a month); free on Sat from 3pm and first Sun of the month; free for under-16s and over-65s; audio guide €3.50; roof terrace €2

Free guided tours first Sun of the month (except Aug; Catalan noon, Spanish 12:15pm), by appointment

▪ The Oval Room has a great café. There's also an elegant restaurant in the Throne Room (first floor).

▪ Enjoy views from the patio by the main entrance and from the roof terrace.

Gallery Guide

The Cambó Bequest, with works by Zurbarán and Goya, and the Thyssen-Bornemisza Collection, with works from the Gothic to the Rococo, are on the ground floor as are the Romanesque works. On the first floor are the modern art galleries and the photography and numismatics collections.

TOP10 ⭐ Parc Güell

Built between 1900 and 1914, Parc Güell was conceived as an English-style garden city, which were becoming popular in the early 20th century. Gaudí's patron, Eusebi Güell, envisaged elegant, artistic villas, gardens and public spaces. However, the project failed. The space was sold to the city and, in 1926, reopened as a public park where Gaudí had let his imagination run riot on the pavilions, stairways, the main square with its sinuous tiled bench and the tiled columns of the marketplace.

Casa del Guarda ④

The porter's lodge, one of two fairy-tale pavilions that guard the park entrance **(right)**, is now an outpost of MUHBA, the Barcelona History Museum *(see p78)*. It contains an exhibition dedicated to the history of Parc Güell.

① Sala Hipòstila

Jujol was one of Gaudí's most gifted collaborators, responsible for decorating the 84 columns **(above)** of the park's marketplace, creating vivid ceiling mosaics from shards of broken tiles.

② Tiled Bench

An enormous bench, which functions as a balustrade, ripples around the edge of Plaça de la Natura. Artists ranging from Miró to Dalí were inspired by its beautiful abstract designs created from colourful broken tiles.

③ Jardins d'Àustria

These beautifully manicured gardens are modern, laid out in the 1970s on what was originally destined to be a plot for a mansion. They are especially lovely in the spring.

⑤ L'Escalinata del Drac

A fountain runs along the length of this impressive, lavishly-tiled staircase, which is topped with whimsical creatures. The most famous of these is the enormous multicoloured dragon, which has become the symbol of Barcelona.

⑥ Viaducts

Gaudí created three viaducts **(below)** to serve as carriageways through Parc Güell. Set into the steep slopes, and supported by archways and columns in the shape of waves or trees, they appear to emerge organically from the hill.

⑦ Plaça de la Natura

The park's main square offers panoramic views across the city, and is fringed by a remarkable tiled bench. The square was originally called the Greek Theatre and was intended for open-air shows, with the audience watching from the surrounding terraces.

8 Pòrtic de la Bugadera

One of the park's many pathways, this is known as the Portico of the Laundress after the woman bearing a basket of washing on her head, which is carved into an arch **(left)**.

Map of Parc Güell

UNFULFILLED IDEAS

Sadly, many of Gaudí's ideas for Parc Güell were never realized owing to the economic failure of Eusebi Güell's garden city. Among the most daring of these ideas was his design for an enormous entrance gate, which he intended to be swung open by a pair of gigantic mechanical gazelles.

10 Turó de les Tres Creus

Three crosses crown the very top of the hill, marking the spot where Gaudí and Güell, both intensely religious men, intended to build Parc Güell's chapel. The climb to the top is well worth it in order to enjoy the spectacular city views.

9 Casa-Museu Gaudí

One of only two houses to be built in Parc Güell, this became Gaudí's home and contains original furnishings and memorabilia. It is located outside the Monumental Zone.

NEED TO KNOW

MAP C1 ■ C/d'Olot s/n ■ 90 220 03 02 (park); 93 256 21 22 (Casa del Guarda) ■ www.parkguell.cat

Open daily Mar: 8:30am–7pm; Apr, Sep & Oct: 8am–8:30pm; May–Aug: 8am–9:30pm; Nov–Feb: 8:30am–6:30pm; last entry 1 hr before closing

Adm to Monumental Zone €7 if bought online, €8 at entrance or from ticket machines; free under 6, €4.90/5.60 under 12; the rest of the park is free of charge; Casa del Guarda included with park ticket; separate ticket required for Casa-Museu Gaudí.

Buy tickets online, from the automatic ticket machines at the park entrance or at the Vallcarca and Lesseps metro stations; admission is timed and you cannot enter outside the time printed on the ticket.

■ It is a good idea to bring a picnic with you. While there is a restaurant in the park, it is expensive and always crowded.

■ Buy a combined MUHBA entrance ticket and get a 21 per cent discount.

■ A combined ticket for the Sagrada Família and Casa-Museu Gaudí is also available.

■ The park has a gift shop as well as a bookshop.

Following pages Elegant Neo-Classical buildings and towering palm trees on Plaça Reial

TOP 10 ⭐ La Pedrera

Completed in 1912, this fantastic, undulating apartment block with its out-of-this-world roof is one of the most emblematic of all Gaudí's works. Casa Milà, also known as La Pedrera ("the stone quarry"), was Gaudí's last great civic work before he dedicated himself to the Sagrada Família. What makes it so magical is that every detail bears the hallmark of Gaudí's visionary genius. Now restored to its former glory, La Pedrera contains the Espai Gaudí, an exhibition hall, courtyards, a roof terrace and the Pedrera Apartment.

1 Façade and Balconies

Defying the laws of gravity, La Pedrera's irreverent curved walls are held in place by undulating horizontal beams attached to invisible girders. Intricate wrought-iron balconies **(below)** are an example of the artisan skill so integral to *Modernisme*.

4 Roof

The strikingly surreal rooftop sculpture park **(right)** has chimneys resembling medieval warriors and huge ventilator ducts twisted into bizarre organic forms **(below)**, not to mention superb views over the Eixample.

2 Espai Gaudí

A series of drawings, photos, maquettes and multimedia displays help visitors grasp Gaudí's architectural wizardry. The museum is housed in the breathtaking vaulted attic, with its 270 catenary brick arches forming atmospheric skeletal corridors.

6 Temporary Exhibition Hall

This gallery space, run by the Catalunya-La Pedrera Foundation, holds regular free art exhibitions. It has shown works by Salvador Dalí, Francis Bacon, Marc Chagall and others. The ceiling **(below)** looks as if it has been coated with whisked egg whites.

3 Interior Courtyard: Carrer Provença

A brigade of guides take the multitude of visitors through here each day. A closer inspection of this first courtyard reveals its beautiful mosaics and multicoloured wall paintings lining a swirling, fairy-tale staircase.

5 Gates

The mastery involved in imagining the huge wrought-iron gates reveals the influence of Gaudí's predecessors – four generations of artisan metal workers. The use of iron is integral to many of Gaudí's edifices.

7 La Pedrera Apartment

This *Modernista* flat **(left)** with period furnishings is a reconstruction of a typical Barcelona bourgeois flat of the late 19th century. It provides an engaging contrast between the sedate middle-class conservatism of the era and the undeniable wackiness of the outer building itself.

8 Interior Courtyard: Passeig de Gràcia

Like the first courtyard, this too has a grand, ornate staircase **(below)**. This one is decorated with a stunning, floral ceiling painting.

9 Auditorium

The auditorium, located in the former coach house, hosts regular events such as jazz and contemporary concerts. The adjacent garden offers visitors a glimpse of greenery.

NEED TO KNOW

MAP E2 ■ Pg de Gràcia 92 ■ 90 220 21 38 ■ wwwlapedrera.com/en

Open 9am–8:30pm daily (to 6:30pm Nov–Feb, 8:30pm at Christmas time); times for evening guided tours and temporary exhibits vary

Adm €22, premium tickets €29 (audio guides in several languages included); advance booking online advised

■ Check the website for information on current activities and temporary exhibitions.

■ Premium tickets let you visit on any day at any time without queuing. You'll have to choose a day and time when booking, but can visit up to 6 months after the chosen date.

■ Tickets for the popular night-time sound and light show can be booked online for €34 (a glass of cava and snacks are included).

Sight Guide
The Espai Gaudí, the Pedrera Apartment, the Passeig de Gràcia and Carrer Provença Courtyards, the Exhibition Room and the roof are open to visitors. A lift goes up to the apartment, Espai Gaudí and the roof. The courtyards, staircases, café and shop are accessible from the entrance on the corner of Pg de Gràcia and C/Provença.

10 La Pedrera Shop and Café

A wide range of Gaudí-related memorabilia includes replicas of the warrior chimneys in ceramic and bronze.

🔟 ⭐ Fundació Joan Miró

Founded in 1975 by Joan Miró himself, who wanted it to be a contemporary arts centre, this is now a superb tribute to a man whose legacy as an artist and a Catalan is visible across the city. The museum holds more than 14,000 of his paintings, sketches and sculptures, tracing Miró's evolution from an innovative Surrealist in the 1920s to one of the world's most challenging modern artists in the 1960s.

Fundació Joan Miró

① L'Estel Matinal

This is one of 23 paintings known as the Constellation Series. The *Morning Star*'s introspective quality reflects Miró's state of mind at the outbreak of World War II, when he was hiding in Normandy. Spindly shapes of birds, women and heavenly bodies are suspended in an empty space.

Pages Catala al Car de Lluna ②

The figurative painting *Catalan Peasant by Moonlight* **(right)** dates from the late 1960s and highlights two of Miró's favourite themes: the earth and the night. The figure of the peasant, a very simple collage of colour, is barely decipherable, as the crescent moon merges with his sickle and the night sky takes on the rich green tones of the earth.

Tapis de la Fundació ③

This immense, richly coloured tapestry **(right)** represents the culmination of Miró's work with textiles, which began during the 1970s.

④ Home i Dona Davant un Munt d'Excrement

Tortured and misshapen semi-abstract figures try to embrace against a black sky. Miró's pessimism at the time of *Man and Woman in Front of a Pile of Excrement* would soon be confirmed by the outbreak of the Civil War.

⑤ Sèrie Barcelona

The Fundació holds the only complete set of prints of this series of 50 black-and-white lithographs. This important collection is only occasionally on display.

⑥ Font de Mercuri

Alexander Calder donated the *Mercury Fountain* to the Fundació as a mark of his friendship with Miró. The work was an anti-fascist tribute, conceived in memory of the attack on the town of Almadén.

8 Terrace Garden

More of Miró's vibrantly colourful and playful sculptures are randomly scattered on a spacious terrace **(left)**, from which you can appreciate city views and the Rationalist architecture of Josep Lluís Sert's geometric building. The 3-m (10-ft) tall *Caress of a Bird* (1967) dominates the terrace.

9 Sculpture Room

This room **(below)** focuses on Miró's sculptures from the 1940s to the 1950s, when he experimented with ceramic, bronze and, later, painted media and found objects. Notable works include *Sun Bird* and *Moon Bird* (both 1946–9).

10 Visiting Exhibitions

Over the years, a number of temporary exhibitions, which are usually held in the Fundació's west wing, have included retrospectives of high-profile artists such as Mark Rothko, Andy Warhol, René Magritte and Fernand Léger.

7 Espai 13

This space showcases the experimental work of new artists from around the world. The exhibitions, which are based on a single theme each year, are usually radical and often make full use of new technologies.

NEED TO KNOW

MAP B4 ▪ Av Miramar, Parc de Montjuïc
▪ 93 443 94 70
▪ www.fmirobcn.org

Open 10am–6pm Tue–Sat (to 8pm Apr–Oct), to 9pm Thu, 8pm Sat, 2:30pm Sun

Adm €12, concessions €7 (two-for-one tickets 6–9pm Thu); Espai 13 €2.50; multimedia guide €5; temporary exhibitions €7

▪ The restaurant-café has a garden terrace with indoor and outdoor seating and is one of the area's best dining options.

▪ In summer, live experimental music is showcased in the auditorium, usually on Thursday nights (but check beforehand).

▪ The gift shop has an original range of Miróesque curiosities, from tablecloths to champagne glasses.

Gallery K. AG
This extension houses 25 paintings on long-term loan from the private collections of members of the Miró family and from Gallery K, founded by Japanese collector Kazumasa Katsuta.

🔟⭐ Museu Picasso

Pay homage to the 20th century's most acclaimed artist at this treasure-filled museum. Highlighting Pablo Picasso's (1881–1973) formative years, the museum boasts the world's largest collection of his early works. At the tender age of 10, Picasso was already revealing remarkable artistic tendencies. In 1895 he moved to Barcelona where he blossomed as an artist. From precocious sketches and powerful family portraits to Blue- and Rose-period works, the museum offers visitors the rare chance to discover the artist as he was discovering himself.

1 Home amb boina

This portrait reveals brush strokes – and a subject matter – that are far beyond a 13-year-old child. No puppies or cats for the young Picasso; instead, he painted the portraits of the oldest men in the village. He signed this work P Ruiz, because at this time he was still using his father's last name.

4 L'Espera (Margot) and La Nana

Picasso's *Margot* is an evocative painting portraying a call girl as she waits for her next customer, while *La Nana* **(left)** captures the defiant expression and stance of a heavily rouged dwarf dancer.

5 El Foll

The Madman is a fine example of Picasso's Blue period. This artistic phase, which lasted from 1901 to 1904, was characterized by melancholic themes and monochromatic, sombre colours.

2 Autoretrat amb perruca

At 14, Picasso painted *Self-portrait with Wig*, a whimsical depiction of how he might have looked during the time of his artistic hero, Velázquez.

3 Ciència i Caritat

One of Picasso's first publicly exhibited paintings was *Science and Charity*. Picasso's father posed as the doctor.

6 Menu de Els Quatre Gats

Picasso's premier Barcelona exhibition was held in 1900 at the Barri Gòtic café and centre of *Modernisme*, Els Quatre Gats. The artist's first commission was the pen-and-ink drawing of himself and a group of artist friends **(left)**, which graced the menu cover of this bohemian hang-out.

7 Arlequí
A lifting of spirits led to Picasso's Neo-Classical period, typified by paintings like *Arlequí* or *The Harlequin* **(left)**, which celebrated the light-hearted liberty of circus performers.

8 Las Meninas Series
Picasso's reverence for Velázquez culminated in this remarkable series of paintings **(below)**, based on the Velázquez painting *Las Meninas*.

9 Home assegnt
Works such as *Seated Man* **(above)** confirmed Picasso's status as the greatest Analytic Cubist painter of the 20th century.

10 Cavall banyegat
The anguished horse in this painting later appears in Picasso's large mural *Guernica*, which reveals the horrors of war. This work gives viewers the chance to observe the process that went into the creation of one of Picasso's most famous paintings.

NEED TO KNOW

MAP P4 ■ C/Montcada 15–23 ■ www.museu picasso.bcn.cat

Open 9am–7pm Tue–Sun, to 9:30pm Thu

Adm €11; temporary exhibitions €3–4.50; combined ticket €14 (book both in advance). Free first Sunday of the month (permanent collections) and 6–9:30pm every Thursday

Guided tours on Sundays (except August) in English at 11am, in Spanish at noon, in Catalan at 1pm; fee included in entrance ticket; book in advance

■ The Museu Picasso is housed in a Gothic palace complex, replete with leafy courtyards, all of which can be explored.

■ The café has outdoor tables in summer and offers a changing menu of daily lunch specials.

Gallery Guide
The museum is housed in five interconnected medieval palaces. The permanent collection is arranged chronologically on the first and second floors of the first three palaces. The last two host temporary exhibitions on the first and second floors.

TOP 10 ★ Palau de la Música Catalana

Barcelona's *Modernista* movement reached its aesthetic peak in Lluís Domènech i Montaner's magnificent 1908 concert hall. The lavish façade is ringed by mosaic pillars, and each part of the foyer in Domènech's "garden of music", from banisters to pillars, has a floral motif. The concert hall, whose height is the same as its breadth, is a celebration of natural forms, capped by a stained-glass dome that floods the space with sunlight.

1 Stained-Glass Ceiling

Topping the concert hall is a breathtaking, stained-glass inverted dome ceiling **(below)**. By day, sunlight streams through the fiery red and orange stained glass, illuminating the hall.

4 Stained-Glass Windows

Blurring the boundaries between the outdoors and the interior, the architect encircled the concert hall with vast stained-glass windows decorated with floral designs that let in sunlight and reveal the changing time of day.

2 Rehearsal Hall of the Orfeó Català

This semicircular, acoustically sound rehearsal room is a smaller version of the massive concert hall one floor above. At its centre is an inlaid foundation stone that commemorates the construction of the Palau.

5 Horse Sculptures

Charging from the ceiling are sculptor Eusebi Aranu's winged horses, infusing the concert hall with movement and verve. Also depicted is a representation of Wagner's chariot ride of the Valkyries, led by galloping horses that leap towards the stage.

6 Façade

The towering façade **(above)** reveals *Modernista* delights on every level. An elaborate mosaic represents the Orfeó Català choral society, founded in 1891.

3 Stage

The semicircular stage **(right)** swarms with activity – even when no one's performing. Eighteen mosaic and terracotta muses spring from the backdrop, playing everything from the harp to the castanets.

7 Foyer and Bar

Modernista architects worked with ceramic, stone, wood, marble and glass, all of which Domènech used liberally, most notably in the opulent foyer and bar.

8 Busts

A bust of Catalan composer Josep Anselm Clavé (1824–74) marks the Palau's commitment to Catalan music. Facing him across the concert hall, a stern, unruly-haired Beethoven **(above)** represents the hall's classical and international repertoire.

9 Lluís Millet Hall

Named after Catalan composer Lluís Millet, this immaculately-preserved lounge boasts gorgeous stained-glass windows. On the main balcony outside are rows of stunning mosaic pillars, each with a different design.

10 Concert and Dance Series

Over 500 concerts and dance shows are staged each year, and seeing a show here is a thrilling experience **(right)**. For symphonic concerts, keep an eye out for the Palau 100 Series; for choral concerts, look out for the Orfeó Català series.

NEED TO KNOW

MAP N2 ■ Sant Pere Més Alt ■ 90 247 54 85 ■ www.palaumusica.cat

Guided tours daily every 30 mins 10am–3:30pm (Easter & Jul: to 6pm; Aug: 9am–6pm); advance booking recommended; tour plus mini recital also available

Adm €18, concessions €11

- ■ Have a pre-concert drink at the *Modernista* stained-glass bar just beyond the foyer.

- ■ There are special concerts for children preceded by kid-friendly guided tours throughout the year.

- ■ Buy tickets online, or from the box office at C/Palau de la Música 4, 90 244 28 82, open 9:30am–9pm Mon–Sat, 9:30am–3pm Sun & two hours before every performance.

ORFEÓ CATALÀ

The famous choral group, Orfeó Català, for whom the concert hall was originally built, performs here regularly and holds a concert on 26 December every year. Book in advance.

TOP 10 ⭐ Museu d'Art Contemporani and Centre de Cultura Contemporània

Barcelona's sleek contemporary art museum stands in bold contrast to its surroundings. The Museu d'Art Contemporani (MACBA), together with the Centre de Cultura Contemporània (CCCB) nearby, has provided a focal point for the city since 1995 and has played an integral part in the rejuvenation of El Raval. MACBA's permanent collection includes big-name Spanish and international artists, while the CCCB serves as a cutting-edge exploration of contemporary culture.

Façade ①
American architect Richard Meier's stark, white, geometrical façade **(right)** makes astartling impression against the backdrop of this dilapidated working-class neighbourhood. Hundreds of panes of glass reflect the skateboarders who gather here daily.

② Visiting Artist's Space
The *raison d'être* of MACBA is this flexible area showing the best in contemporary art. Past exhibitions have included Zush and acclaimed painter Dieter Roth.

③ Revolving Permanent Collection
The permanent collection comprises over 2,000 – mostly European – modern artworks, 10 per cent of which are on show at any one time. All major contemporary artistic trends are represented. This 1974 work **(below)** by Eduardo Arranz Bravo is titled *Homea*.

④ Interior Corridors
Space and light are omnipresent in the bare white walkways that hover between floors **(left)**. Look through the glass panels onto the Plaça dels Àngels for myriad images before you even enter the gallery spaces.

6 A Sudden Awakening

One of the only pieces of art on permanent display is Antoni Tàpies' deconstructed bed (1992–3), with its bedding flung across the wall in disarray **(left)**. Its presence to the right of the main entrance underlines the late Tàpies' importance in the world of Catalan modern art.

5 Capella MACBA

One of the few surviving Renaissance chapels in Barcelona has been converted for use as MACBA's temporary exhibition space. It is located in a former convent across the Plaça dels Àngels *(see p87)*.

7 Thinking and Reading Spaces

Pleasant and unusual features of MACBA are the white leather sofas between the galleries. Usually next to a shelf of relevant books and a set of headphones, these quiet spaces provide the perfect resting spot to contemplate – and learn more about – the art.

8 Temporary Exhibitions/ CCCB

Exhibitions at the CCCB – unlike at MACBA – tend to be more theme-based than artist-specific. Home to the World Press Photo exhibition in November, a festival of cinema shorts in September, and avant-garde art exhibits, the CCCB is always at the forefront of the latest cultural trends.

El Pati de les Dones/CCCB 9

This courtyard **(right)** off Carrer Montalegre forms part of the neighbouring CCCB. An ultramodern prismatic screen acts as a mirror reflecting the medieval courtyard, giving visitors a magical juxtaposition of different architectural styles.

10 Plaça Joan Coromines

The contrast between the modern MACBA, the University building, the Tuscan-style CCCB and the 19th-century mock-Romanesque church make this square one of the city's most enchanting. It is home to the terrace restaurants of MACBA and CCCB.

NEED TO KNOW

MACBA: MAP K2 ▪ Pl dels Àngels ▪ 93 412 08 10 ▪ www.macba.cat/en

Open 11am–8pm Mon, Wed & Fri, 10am–9pm Thu, 10am–7:30pm Sat, 10am–3pm Sun

Adm €10 (all exhibitions and Experience MACBA); free for under-14s and over-65s

CCCB: Map K1 ▪ C/Montalegre 5 ▪ 93 306 41 00 ▪ www.cccb.org/en

Open 11am–8pm Tue–Sun

Adm €6 for 1 show, €8 for 2 shows; concessions €4 for 1 show, €6 for 2 shows; free for under-12s; free every Sunday 3–8pm

▪ Pause at the nearby Plaça dels Àngels café (C/Ferlandina), which offers nouvelle/Catalan food to a hip crowd, or at CCCB's C3 Bar.

▪ MACBA offers tours in sign language as well as adapted tours for the visually impaired.

Sights Guide

Although they share the Plaça Joan Coromines, MACBA and CCCB have separate entrances. Both multilevel galleries have flexible display spaces. MACBA has rest areas dotted among the galleries on all floors, allowing you to take breaks as you explore.

The Top 10
of Everything

**Museu d'Art Contemporani and
Centre de Cultura Contemporània**

Moments in History

1 3rd Century BC: The Founding of a City

Barcino, as the city was first known, was founded in the 3rd century BC by Carthaginian Hamilcar Barca. It was taken by the Romans in 218 BC but played second fiddle in the region to the provincial capital of Tarragona.

2 4th–11th Centuries: Early Invasions

As the Roman Empire began to fall apart in the 5th century, Visigoths from the Toulouse area took over the city. They were followed in the 8th century by the Moors, who moved up through the Iberian peninsula at great speed. Around AD 800, Charlemagne conquered the area with the help of the Pyrenean counts, bringing it back under the control of the Franks.

Exhibition poster, 1929

3 12th–16th Centuries: The Middle Ages

During this period, Barcelona was the capital of a Catalan empire that stretched across the Mediterranean. The city's fortune was built on commerce, but as neighbouring Castile expanded into the New World, trading patterns shifted and the Catalan dynasty faltered. Barcelona fell into decline and came under Castilian domination.

4 1638–1652: Catalan Revolt

In reaction to the oppressive policies set out in Madrid, now ruled by the Austrian Habsburgs, various local factions, known as *Els Segadors*, rebelled. Fighting began in 1640 and dragged on until 1652, when the Catalans and their French allies were finally defeated.

5 19th Century: Industry and Prosperity

Booming industry and trade with the Americas brought activity to the city. Immigrants poured in from the countryside, laying the foundations of prosperity but also seeds of unrest. The old city walls came down, broad Eixample avenues were laid out and workers crowded into the old city neighbourhoods left behind by the middle classes.

6 1888–1929: The Renaixença

This new wealth, showcased in the International Exhibitions of 1888 and 1929, sparked a Catalan renaissance. *Modernista* mansions sprouted up and the nationalist bourgeoisie oversaw a revival of Catalan culture.

7 1909–1931: The Revolutionary Years

Discontent was brewing among workers, Catalan nationalists, communists, Spanish fascists, royalists, anarchists and republicans. In 1909, protests against the Moroccan war turned into a brutal riot, the *Setmana Tràgica* (Tragic Week). Lurching towards Civil War, Catalonia suffered under a dictatorship before being declared a republic in 1931.

8 1936–1975: Civil War and Franco

At the outbreak of war in 1936, Barcelona's workers and militants

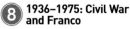

managed to fend off General Franco's troops for a while. The city was taken by Fascist forces in 1939, prompting a wave of repression, particularly of the Catalan language, which was banned in schools.

Franco addressing a rally, 1939

⑨ 1975–1980s: Transition to Democracy

Franco's death in 1975 paved the way for democracy. The Catalan language was rehabilitated and the region was granted autonomy. The first Catalan government was elected in 1980.

⑩ 1992–Present Day: The Olympics and Beyond

Barcelona was catapulted onto the world stage in 1992 with the highly successful Olympic Games. In 2015, the Junts pel Sí ('Together for Yes') coalition won the Catalan regional elections and in 2017, they held an independence referendum which was decreed illegal by the Spanish state.

Opening ceremony, 1992 Olympics

TOP 10 HISTORICAL FIGURES

Ferdinand the Catholic

1 Guifré the Hairy
The first Count of Barcelona (d. 897), seen as Catalonia's founding father.

2 Ramon Berenguer IV
He united Catalonia and joined it with Aragon by marrying the Aragonese princess Petronilla in 1137.

3 Jaume I the Conqueror
This 13th-century warrior-king conquered the Balearics and Valencia, laying the foundations for the empire.

4 Ramon Llull
Mallorcan philosopher and missionary, Llull (d. 1316) is the greatest figure in medieval Catalan literature.

5 Ferdinand the Catholic
King of Aragon and Catalonia (d.1516), he married Isabella of Castile, paving the way for the formation of a united Spain and the end of Catalan independence.

6 Idlefons Cerdà
The 19th-century urban planner who designed the Eixample.

7 Antoni Gaudí
An idiosyncratic and devout *Modernista* architect, Gaudí was responsible for Barcelona's most famous monuments.

8 Francesc Macià
This socialist nationalist politician proclaimed the birth of the Catalan Republic in 1931 and Catalan regional autonomy in 1932.

9 Lluís Companys
Catalan president during the Civil War. Exiled in France, he was arrested by the Gestapo in 1940 and returned to Franco, who had him executed.

10 Ada Colau
A street activist turned politician, he is now the popular, charismatic and controversial mayor of Barcelona.

Churches and Chapels

1 Barcelona Cathedral
Barcelona's magnificent Gothic cathedral boasts an eye-catching façade and a peaceful cloister (see pp18–19).

2 Església de Santa Maria del Mar
The elegant church of Santa Maria del Mar (1329–83) is one of the finest examples of Catalan Gothic, a style characterized by simplicity. A spectacular stained-glass rose window illuminates the lofty interior (see pp78–9).

Rose window, Església de Santa Maria del Mar

3 Capella de Sant Miquel and Església al Monestir de Pedralbes
Accessed through an arch set in ancient walls, the lovely Monestir de Pedralbes (see p117), founded in 1327, still has the air of a closed community. Inside is a Gothic cloister and the Capella de Sant Miquel, decorated with murals by Catalan artist Ferrer Bassa in 1346. The adjoining Gothic church contains the alabaster tomb of Queen Elisenda, the monastery's founder – on the church side, her effigy wears royal robes; on the other, a nun's habit.

4 Església de Sant Pau del Camp
Founded as a Benedictine monastery in the 9th century by Guifre II, a count of Barcelona, this church was rebuilt the following century. Its sculpted façade and intimate cloister with rounded arches exemplify the Romanesque style (see p89).

5 Església de Sant Pere de les Puelles
MAP P2 ▪ Pl de Sant Pere ▪ Open 9am–1pm & 5–7:45pm Mon–Fri, 9am–1pm & 4:30–6pm Sat, 11am–1:15pm Sun

Built in 801 as a chapel for troops stationed in Barcelona, this església later became a spiritual retreat for young noblewomen. The church was rebuilt in the 1100s and is notable for its Romanesque central cupola and a series of capitals with carved leaves. Look out for two stone tablets depicting a Greek cross, which are from the original chapel.

6 Temple Expiatori del Sagrat Cor
MAP B1 ▪ Pl del Tibidabo ▪ 93 417 56 86 ▪ Open Nov–Feb: 11am–6pm (to 7pm Mar–May & Oct; to 8pm Jun–Sep) ▪ Adm for lifts

Mount Tibidabo is an appropriate perch for this huge, over-the-top Neo-Gothic church, topped with a large golden statue of Christ with arms outstretched. The name Tibidabo comes from the words *tibidabo*, meaning "I shall give you", said to have been uttered by the Devil in his temptation of Christ. Zealously serving the devoted, the priest here celebrates the Eucharist throughout the day (see p119).

Temple Expiatori del Sagrat Cor

7 Església de Santa Maria del Pi

MAP L3 ▪ Pl del Pi ▪ Open 9:30am–8:30pm daily ▪ Adm 5–6pm ▪ DA

This lovely Gothic church with its ornate stained-glass windows graces the Plaça del Pi *(see p47)*.

8 Capella de Santa Àgata

MAP N3 ▪ Pl del Rei ▪ Open 10am–7pm Tue–Sat, 10am–8pm Sun ▪ Adm (free 3–8pm Sun)

Within the beautiful Palau Reial is the medieval Capella de Santa Àgata, which can only be entered as part of a visit to the Museu d'Història de Barcelona *(see p78)*. The 15th-century altarpiece is by Jaume Huguet.

9 Capella de Sant Jordi

MAP M4 ▪ Pl Sant Jaume ▪ Guided tours 10:30am–1:30pm second and fourth Sat and Sun of the month; reservations essential

Inside the Palau de la Generalitat *(see p77)* is this fine 15th-century chapel, dedicated to the patron saint of Catalonia.

Interior of the Església de Betlem

10 Església de Betlem

MAP L3 ▪ C/Xuclà 2 ▪ Open 8:30am–1:30pm & 6–9pm daily ▪ DA

La Rambla *(see pp16–17)* was once dotted with religious buildings, most built in the 17th and 18th centuries when the Catholic Church was flush with money. This Baroque *església* is one of the major functioning churches from this period.

TOP 10 CATALAN SAINTS AND VIRGINS

The famous Virgin of Montserrat

1 Virgin of Montserrat
The famous "Black Virgin" is a patron saint of Catalonia, along with Sant Jordi.

2 Sant Jordi
Catalonia's patron saint is St George, whose dragon-slaying prowess is depicted all over the city.

3 Virgin Mercè
The Virgin of Mercè became a patron saint of the city in 1687, and shares the honour with Santa Eulàlia. The most raucous festival in town is the popular Festes de la Mercè *(see p72)*.

4 Santa Eulàlia
Santa Eulàlia is Barcelona's co-patron saint (with La Mercè). She was martyred by the Romans in around AD 300.

5 Santa Elena
Legend has it that St Helena converted to Christianity after finding Christ's cross in Jerusalem in AD 346.

6 Santa Llúcia
The patron saint of eyes and vision is celebrated on 13 December, when the blind come to worship at the Santa Llúcia chapel in Barcelona Cathedral *(see pp18–19)*.

7 Sant Cristòfor
Cars are blessed on the feast day of Sant Cristòfor, patron saint of travellers, at a tiny chapel on C/Regomir *(see p80)*.

8 Sant Antoni de Padua
On 13 June, those seeking a husband or wife pray to the patron saint of love.

9 Santa Rita
Those searching for miracles pray to Santa Rita, deliverer of the impossible.

10 Sant Joan
The night of St John *(see p72)* is celebrated with bonfires and fireworks.

⭐🔟 Museums and Galleries

The modern buildings of the Fundació Joan Miró

Fundació Joan Miró

The airy, high-ceilinged galleries of this splendid museum are a fitting home for the bold, abstract works of Joan Miró, one of Catalonia's most acclaimed 20th-century artists (see pp28–9).

2 Museu Nacional d'Art de Catalunya

Discover Catalonia's Romanesque and Gothic heritage at this impressive museum, housed in the 1929 Palau Nacional. Highlights include striking medieval frescoes and a collection of *Modernista* furnishings and artworks (see pp20–21).

3 Museu Picasso

Witness the budding – and meteoric rise – of Picasso's artistic genius at this unique museum, one of the world's largest collections of the painter's early works (see pp30–31).

4 Museu d'Art Contemporani & Centre de Cultura Contemporània

Inaugurated in 1995, MACBA is Barcelona's centre for modern art. Combined with the neighbouring CCCB, the two buildings form an artistic and cultural hub in the heart of El Raval. Both regularly host temporary exhibitions: the MACBA showcases contemporary artists; the CCCB is more theme-based (see pp34–5).

5 Fundació Tàpies

Works by Catalan artist Antoni Tàpies are showcased in this graceful *Modernista* building. Venture inside to discover Tàpies' rich repertoire, from early collage works to large abstract paintings, many alluding to political and social themes (see p108).

6 Museu d'Història de Barcelona (MUHBA)

Explore the medieval Palau Reial and wander among the splendid remains of Barcelona's Roman walls and waterways at the city's history museum. The museum is partly housed in the 15th-century Casa Padellàs on the impressive medieval Plaça del Rei (see p78).

FC Barcelona badge

7 Museu del FC Barcelona

This shrine to the city's football club draws a mind-boggling number of fans. Trophies, posters and other memorabilia celebrate the club's 100-year history. Also visit the adjacent Camp Nou Stadium (see p118).

⑧ Museu Frederic Marès

Catalan sculptor Frederic Marès (1893–1991) was a passionate and eclectic collector. Housed here, under one roof, are many remarkable finds amassed during his travels. Among the vast array of historical objects on display are Romanesque and Gothic religious art and sculptures, plus everything from dolls and fans to pipes and walking sticks (see p78).

⑨ Museu Marítim

The formidable seafaring history of Barcelona is showcased in the cavernous, 13th-century Drassanes Reials (Royal Shipyards). The collection, which ranges from the Middle Ages to the 19th century, includes a full-scale replica of the *Real*, the flagship galley of Don Juan of Austria, who led the Christians to victory against the Turks at the Battle of Lepanto in 1571. Also on display are model ships, maps and navigational instruments (see p87).

Medieval warship, Museu Marítim

⑩ CosmoCaixa Museu de la Ciència

Exhibits covering the whole history of science, from the Big Bang to the computer age, are housed in this modern museum. Highlights include an interactive tour of the geological history of our planet, an area of real Amazonian rainforest, and a planetarium. There are also temporary displays on environmental issues (see p118) and family activities.

TOP 10 QUIRKY MUSEUMS AND MONUMENTS

Wax models at the Museu de Cera

1 Museu de Cera
MAP L5 ▪ Ptge de la Banca 7
Home to over 350 wax figures, from Marilyn Monroe to Franco and Gaudí.

2 Can Framis
MAP H4 ▪ C/Roc Borronat 116–126
Excellent museum of Catalan contemporary art in an 18th-century factory.

3 Centre d'Interpretació del Call
MAP M4 ▪ Pl de Manuel Ribé
Artifacts from Barcelona's medieval Jewish community.

4 Museu de Cultures del Món
MAP P4 ▪ Carrer Montcada 12
Objects of artistic and cultural heritage from the people of Africa, Asia, America and Oceania.

5 Museu dels Autòmates
MAP B1 ▪ Parc d'Atraccions del Tibidabo
A colourful museum of human and animal automatons.

6 Museu de la Xocolata
MAP P4 ▪ C/Comerç 36
A celebration of chocolate; interactive exhibits, edible city models and tastings.

7 Museu del Disseny
MAP H3 ▪ Pl de les Glòries Catalanes
A design museum covering clothes, architecture, objects and graphic design.

8 Museu del Perfum
MAP E2 ▪ Pg de Gràcia 39
Hundreds of perfume bottles from Roman times to the present.

9 Cap de Barcelona
MAP N5 ▪ Pg de Colom
Pop artist Roy Lichtenstein's "Barcelona Head" (1992).

10 Peix
MAP G5 ▪ Port Olímpic
Frank Gehry's huge shimmering fish sculpture (1992).

ᴛᴏᴘ10 Modernista Buildings

music. Ablaze with mosaic friezes, stained glass, ceramics and sculptures, it displays the full glory of the *Modernista* style. The work of Miquel Blay on the façade is rated as one of the best examples of *Modernista* sculpture in Barcelona (see pp32–3).

4 Fundació Tàpies

With a Rationalist, plain façade alleviated only by its *Mudéjar*-style brickwork, this austere building (see p108), dating from 1886, was originally home to the publishing house Montaner i Simón. It bears the distinction of being the first *Modernista* work to be designed by Domènech i Montaner, which explains why it has so few of the ornate decorative touches that distinguish his later works. Today it is home to the Fundació Tàpies, and is dominated by an enormous sculpture by the Catalan artist.

5 Sant Pau Recinte Modernista

In defiant contrast to the Eixample's symmetrical grid-like pattern, this ambitious project (see p107) was planned around two avenues running at 45-degree angles to the Eixample streets. Started by Domènech i Montaner in 1905 and completed by his son in 1930, the Hospital de la Santa Creu i de Sant Pau's pavilions are lavishly embellished

1 Sagrada Família

Dizzying spires and intricate sculptures adorn Gaudí's magical masterpiece. Construction began at the height of *Modernisme*, but is still in progress more than a century later (see pp12–15).

2 La Pedrera

This amazing apartment block, with its curving façade and bizarre rooftop, has all of Gaudí's architectural trademarks. Especially characteristic are the building's wrought-iron balconies and the ceramic mosaics decorating the entrance halls (see pp26–7).

3 Palau de la Música Catalana

Domènech i Montaner's magnificent concert hall is a joyous celebration of Catalan

Hospital de la Santa Creu i de Sant Pau

Colourful exterior of Casa Batlló

with mosaics, stained glass, and sculptures by Eusebi Arnau. The octagonal columns with floral capitals are inspired by those in the Monestir de Santes Creus (see p128), to the south of Barcelona.

6 Casa Amatller
■ MAP E2 ■ Pg de Gràcia 41
■ Open 11am–7pm daily; guided tours only; check timings online
■ Adm ■ www.fundacionamatller.org

The top of Casa Amatller's façade bursts into a brilliant display of blue, cream and pink tiles with burgundy florets. Architect Puig i Cadafalch's exaggerated decorative use of ceramics is typical of the *Modernisme* style. Tours include the *Modernista* apartment and a slide show in Amatller's former photography studio, and describe the neo-medieval vestibule (see p107).

7 Casa de les Punxes (Casa Terrades)

Taking *Modernisme*'s Gothic and medieval obsession to extremes that others seldom dared, Puig i Cadafalch created this imposing, castle-like structure between 1903 and 1905 (see p108). Given the nickname Casa de les Punxes or the "House of Spines" because of the sharp, needle-like spires that rise up from its conical turrets, the building's real name is Casa Terrades, for its original owners. The flamboyant spires contrast with a façade that is, by *Modernista* standards, sparsely decorated.

8 Casa Batlló
■ MAP E2 ■ Pg de Gràcia 43
■ Open 9am–9pm daily ■ Adm (audio guide) ■ www.casabatllo.es

Illustrating Gaudí's nationalist sentiments, Casa Batlló, on La Mansana de la Discòrdia (see p107), is a representation of the Sant Jordi story (see p41). The roof is the dragon's back; the balconies, in the form of carnival masks, are the skulls of the dragon's victims. The façade exemplifies Gaudí's remarkable use of colour and texture.

9 Casa Lleó Morera
■ MAP E3 ■ Pg de Gràcia 35
■ www.casalleomorera.com

Ironwork, ceramics, sculpture and stained glass come together here in a synthesis of the decorative and fine arts. The building's exterior, designed by architect Domenèch i Montaner, can be viewed from the street. Only the ground floor is currently open to the public, occupied by the luxury leather-goods maker Loewe.

10 Palau Güell

This is a fine example of Gaudí's experiments with structure, especially the use of parabolic arches to orchestrate space. He also used unusual building materials, such as ebony and rare South American woods (see p87).

Arched interiors of Palau Güell

TOP 10 **Perfect Squares**

Stately Plaça Reial, surrounded by Neo-Classical buildings and palm trees

① Plaça Reial
The arcaded Plaça Reial, in the heart of the Barri Gòtic, is unique among Barcelona's squaresß with its old-world charm, gritty urbanization and Neo-Classical flair. It is home not only to Gaudí lampposts and majestic mid-19th-century buildings, but also a slew of happening bars and clubs, and an entertaining and very colourful crowd of inner-city Barcelona denizens (see p78).

② Plaça de Catalunya
MAP M1
Barcelona's nerve centre is the huge Plaça de Catalunya, a lively hub from which the city's activity seems to radiate. This square is most visitors' first real glimpse of Barcelona. The

airport bus stops here, as do RENFE trains and countless metro and bus lines, including most night buses. The square's commercial swagger is evident all around, headed by Spain's omnipresent department store, El Corte Inglés (see p66). Pigeons flutter chaotically at the square's centre and hordes of travellers – from backpackers to tour groups – wander about. The main tourist information office is here. Concerts are held in the square during festivals.

③ Plaça del Rei
MAP N4
One of the city's best-preserved medieval squares, the Barri Gòtic's Plaça del Rei is ringed by grand buildings. Among them is the 14th-century Palau Reial (see p78), which houses the Saló del Tinell, a spacious Catalan Gothic throne room and banqueting hall.

④ Plaça de Sant Jaume
Laden with power and history, this is the administrative heart of modern-day Barcelona. The *plaça* is flanked by the city's two key government buildings, the stately Palau de la Generalitat and the 15th-century Ajuntament (see p77).

Plaça de Catalunya

⑤ Plaça de la Vila de Gràcia
MAP F1

The progressive, bohemian area of Gràcia, a former village annexed by Barcelona in 1897, still exudes a small-town ambience where socializing with the neighbours means heading for the nearest *plaça*. Topping the list is this atmospheric square, with an impressive clock tower rising at its centre. Bustling outdoor cafés draw buskers and a sociable crowd.

⑥ Plaça de Sant Josep Oriol and Plaça del Pi
MAP M3 & M4

Old-world charm meets café culture in the Barri Gòtic's leafy Plaça de Sant Josep Oriol and Plaça del Pi, named after the pine trees (*pi* in Catalan) that shade its nooks and crannies. The lovely Gothic church of Santa Maria del Pi (see p41) is set between the two squares.

⑦ Plaça Comercial
MAP P4

The buzzy Passeig del Born culminates in Plaça Comercial, an inviting square dotted with cafés and bars. It faces the 19th-century Born Market (see p78), which has been transformed into a cultural centre and exhibition space.

⑧ Plaça de Santa Maria
MAP N5

The magnificent Església de Santa Maria del Mar (see p78) imbues its namesake *plaça*, in the El Born

Cafés on Plaça de Santa Maria

district, with a certain spiritual calm. Bask in its Gothic ambience, people watch, and soak up the sun at one of the outdoor terrace cafés.

⑨ Plaça del Sol
MAP F1

Tucked within the cosy grid of Gràcia, this square is surrounded by handsome 19th-century buildings. As evening descends, it becomes one of the most lively spots for nighttime festivities and you can join all the *Barcelonins* who come here to mingle on the outdoor terraces.

⑩ Plaça de la Vila de Madrid
MAP M2

Mere steps from La Rambla (see pp16–17) is this spacious *plaça*, graced with the remains of a Roman necropolis. A remnant of Roman Barcino, the square sat just beyond the boundaries of the walled Roman city. A row of unadorned 2nd to 4th-century tombs was discovered here in 1957. The complete remains can be viewed from street level.

🔟 Parks and Beaches

① Parc de la Ciutadella

MAP R4 ▪ Pg Pujades ▪ Open 10am–10:30pm; zoo timings vary, check website ▪ Adm (for the zoo) ▪ www.zoobarcelona.cat/en

The largest landscaped park in Barcelona offers a green, tranquil antidote to city life. Once the location of the 18th-century military citadel, this lovely, serene 19th-century park is now home to the city zoo, the Catalan parliament, a placid boating lake and a variety of works by Catalan sculptors as well as modern artists. It also has the flamboyant Cascada fountain, which Gaudí helped design.

Cascada fountain, Parc de la Ciutadella

② Parc Güell

The twisting pathways and avenues of columned arches of Parc Güell blend in with the hillside, playfully fusing nature and fantasy. From the esplanade, with its stunning mosaic bench, visitors have spectacular views of the city and of the fairy-tale gatehouses below (see pp22–3).

③ Parc del Laberint d'Horta

Dating back to 1791, these enchanting gardens are among the city's oldest. Situated above the city, where the air is cooler and cleaner, the park includes themed gardens, waterfalls and a small canal. The highlight is the vast maze with a statue of Eros at its centre (see p118).

Vibrant mosaic at Parc Güell

④ Parc de Cervantes

Av Diagonal 708 ▪ Open 10am–dusk

Built in 1964 to celebrate 25 years of Franco's rule, this beautiful park on the outskirts of the city would have been more appropriately named Park of the Roses. There are over 11,000 rose bushes of 245 varieties; when in bloom, their scent pervades the park. People pour in at weekends, but the park is blissfully deserted during the week.

⑤ Jardins del Palau de Pedralbes

Av Diagonal 686 ▪ Open 10am–dusk

These picturesque gardens lie just in front of the former Palau Reial (royal palace) of Pedralbes. Under an

Parc del Laberint d'Horta

enormous eucalyptus tree, near a small bamboo forest, is the Fountain of Hercules with a wrought-iron dragon-head spout by Gaudí which was only discovered in 1984.

6 Parc de Joan Miró
MAP B2 ■ C/Tarragona 74
■ Open 10am–11pm

Also known as Parc de l'Escorxador, this park was built on the site of a 19th-century slaughterhouse (*escorxador*). Dominating the paved upper level of the park is Miró's striking 22-m (72-ft) sculpture, *Dona i Ocell (Woman and Bird)*, created in 1983. There are several play areas for kids and a couple of kiosk cafés.

7 Parc de l'Espanya Industrial
C/Muntadas 37 ■ Open 10am–midnight

Located on the site of a former textile factory, this modern park was built in 1986 by Basque architect Luis Peña Ganchegui. It is an appealing space, with 10 lighthouse-style viewing towers along one side of the boating lake and an enormous cast-iron dragon that doubles as a slide. There is a good terrace bar with a playground for kids.

8 City Beaches
The beaches of Barcelona were once insalubrious areas to be avoided. With the 1992 Olympics they underwent a radical facelift and today the stretches of Barceloneta and the Port Olímpic are a people magnet. A short hop on the metro from the city centre, the beaches are regularly cleaned and the facilities include showers, toilets, play areas for kids, volleyball nets and an open-air gym. Boats and surfboards can be hired. Be aware, though, that bag snatching is endemic (see p101).

Castelldefels beach

9 Castelldefels
Train to Platja de Castelldefels from Estació de Sants or Passeig de Gràcia

Just 20 km (12 miles) south of Barcelona are 5 km (3 miles) of wide sandy beaches with shallow waters. Beach bars entice weekend sun worshippers out of the afternoon sun for long, lazy seafood lunches and jugs of sangria. Windsurfers are available for hire.

10 Premià de Mar and El Masnou
Train to Premià or El Masnou from Plaça de Catalunya or Estació de Sants

Arguably the best beaches within easy reach of Barcelona, just 20 km (12 miles) to the north of the city, these two adjoining beaches lure locals with golden sand and clear, blue waters.

🔟 Off the Beaten Track

Dragon, Güell Pavilions gate

1 Güell Pavilions

MAP B2 ▪ Av Pedralbes 7 ▪ 93 317 76 52 ▪ Open 10am–4pm daily; phone in advance for guided visits (Spanish and Catalan only) ▪ Adm

Gaudí designed the gatehouses and stable, known collectively as the Güell Pavilions, for his patron Eusebi Güell in the 1880s. You can admire the enormous dragon which lunges out of the wrought-iron gate, and visit the complex as part of a guided tour. One of the gatehouses is now a branch of the Museu d'Història de Barcelona (see p78).

2 Jardins de la Rambla de Sants

MAP A2 ▪ C/d'Antoni de Capmany s/n

This elevated park, which stretches for almost a kilometre from the Plaça de Sants to the La Bordeta district, is built above a disused railway track. It provides a peaceful stroll, with some refreshing bursts of greenery, in amongst the high-rise apartment blocks and old factory buildings.

3 El Refugi 307

MAP C5 ▪ C/Nou de la Rambla 175 ▪ 93 256 21 22 ▪ Guided tours at 10:30am (in English) on Sundays, and by prior arrangement ▪ Adm ▪ www.barcelona.cat/museu historia/en

More than a thousand underground shelters were built beneath the city during the Spanish Civil War, when Barcelona was under bombardment by the nationalist forces. Shelter 307, with 400 m (1,312 ft) of tunnels, contained an infirmary, a toilet, a water fountain, a fireplace and a children's room. It is now part of the Museu d'Història de Barcelona (see p78) and provides a fascinating glimpse into the misery endured by city residents during the war.

4 Mercat de la Llibertat

Pl Llibertat 27 ▪ 93 217 09 95

The Mercat de la Llibertat in Gràcia was built in 1888 and is notable for its beautiful wrought-iron and ceramic decoration. As well as a fabulous range of fresh produce, it also boasts some excellent stalls selling everything from original photographs to fashions.

5 Parc del Laberint d'Horta

These lovely 18th-century gardens are filled with classical statuary, little pavilions and ornamental ponds, but it is the fabulous – and surprisingly tricky – maze at their heart that is the big draw (see p118).

Pavilion, Parc del Laberint d'Horta

6 Bunkers del Carmel

MAP C1 ▪ C/del Turó de la Rovira s/n

Barcelona has a handful of disused bunkers – a reminder of the aerial attacks that took place during Spain's long civil war. Chiselled into the side of a hill in the working-class El Carmel district, the roof of this bunker acts as a viewing platform.

It's become a popular place to enjoy a few beers and contemplate the city's skyline as the sun goes down.

7 Basílica de la Puríssima Concepció

MAP F2 ▪ C/d'Aragó 299 ▪ Open 7:30am–1pm & 5–9pm Mon–Fri (cloister entrance); 1–5pm Mon–Fri (Chapel Montserrat); 7:30am–2pm & 5–9pm Sun ▪ www.parroquia concepciobcn.org

Dating back to the 13th century, this basilica was originally part of the Santa Maria de Jonqueres monastery. It was moved stone by stone to its current site in the 19th century. Head for the charming Gothic cloister, which is filled with greenery and birdsong, and bordered by slender 15th-century columns. The basilica regularly hosts concerts.

8 Convent de Sant Agustí

MAP F4 ▪ Pl l'Academia s/n, C/Comerç 36 ▪ 93 256 50 17 ▪ Open 9am–10pm Mon–Fri, 10am–2pm & 4–9pm Sat ▪ Café: lunchtime Tue–Sat

The 15th-century Convent de Sant Agustí is now a cultural centre, with a lovely little café underneath the arches of what remains of the cloister. Relaxed and family-friendly, it is a great place to spend an afternoon.

9 Plaça Osca

MAP B2

This lovely, leafy old square in the Sants neighbourhood is flanked by cafés and bars, with tables spilling out onto the pavements. Rarely frequented by tourists but increasingly popular with trendy locals, it boasts a clutch of great spots to enjoy artisan beers and organic tapas.

10 Parc de Cervantes

Every spring, hundreds of people converge on the gardens in the Parc de Cervantes to admire the blooms of 11,000 rose bushes of 245 varieties. Grassy lawns extend around the rose gardens, dotted with picnic areas and children's playgrounds (see p48).

The lush lawns and rose bushes of the Parc de Cervantes

Attractions for Children

Enjoying a ride at the Parc d'Atraccions del Tibidabo

1 Parc d'Atraccions del Tibidabo

With its old-fashioned rides, the only surviving funfair in the city is a delight (see p117). The attractions include a roller coaster, a House of Horrors, bumper cars, a Ferris wheel and the Museu dels Autòmates (see p43), with animatronics of all shapes and sizes. There's also a puppet show, picnic areas, playgrounds and plenty of bars and restaurants.

2 Parc Zoològic

The zoo in the Ciutadella park (see p48) has an enormous adventure playground where children can run wild. There are also dolphin shows in one of the aquariums. Other activities for children include guided tours and workshops. The "farm" area has goats and rabbits that younger children can stroke.

3 Museu Marítim

Ancient maps showing monster-filled seas, restored fishing boats and a collection of ships' figureheads give a taste of the city's maritime history. Well worth a look is the full-size Spanish galleon complete with sound and light effects. Set in the vast former medieval shipyards, the Drassanes, this museum is an absolute must for any budding sea captain (see p87).

4 L'Aquàrium de Barcelona

One of Europe's biggest aquariums, this underwater kingdom is made up of 21 enormous tanks brimming with nearly 400 marine species. The highlight of a visit here is the Oceanari, where a walk-through glass tunnel will bring you face to face with three huge grey sharks named Drake, Morgan and Maverick, lurking in 4.5 million litres (990,000 gallons) of water (see p101).

Parc del Laberint d'Horta maze

5 Parc del Laberint d'Horta

The main feature of this exceptional park is the huge hedge maze where children can live out their *Alice in Wonderland* fantasies. Unfulfilled expectations of Mad Hatters are made up for by an enormous play area and a bar for the grown-ups, by the park entrance. The park is particularly busy on Sundays *(see p118)*.

6 Telefèric de Montjuïc

MAP C5 ■ Parc de Montjuïc ■ Open Mar–May & mid-Sep–Oct: 10:30am–7pm; Jun–mid-Sep: 10:30am–8pm; Nov–Mar: 11am–5:30pm daily ■ Adm

Instead of taking the nerve-jangling cable-car ride across the port, try these smaller, lower-altitude cable-car trips if you have children with you. The ride to the Montjuïc summit also has the added appeal of the castle *(see p95)* at the top, with cannons for the kids to clamber on.

7 La Rambla

Your shoulders will be aching from carrying the kids high above the crowds by the time you reach the end of Barcelona's main boulevard *(see pp16–17)*. Fire eaters, buskers, human statues dressed up as Greek goddesses – you name it and it's likely to be keeping the hordes entertained on La Rambla. Put a coin in the human statue's hat and be rewarded with a sudden move, or, if you're a child, the gift of a tiny lollipop.

Human statue, La Rambla

8 City Beaches

For kids, there's more to going to the beach in Barcelona than just splashing in warm waters and frolicking in the sand. The Port Vell and Port Olímpic *platges* (beaches) offer a good choice of well-equipped play areas to keep the little ones entertained. Numerous bars and restaurants make finding refreshment easy too *(see p101)*.

9 Museu d'Història de Catalunya

This child-friendly museum traces Catalonia's history through a range of dynamic, interactive exhibits. The best of these allows visitors to get dressed up as medieval knights and gallop around on wooden horses. Very popular with Catalan school groups, the museum is equally enjoyable for visitors of all ages. As well as other children's activities, every Saturday it hosts a story hour when Catalan legends are re-enacted *(see p101)*.

10 Boat Trips

The city's "swallow boats", Las Golondrinas *(see p102)*, make regular trips out of the port, providing a fun excursion for older children. Younger kids, however, will probably prefer messing about in a rowing boat on the lake at the Parc de la Ciutadella *(see p48)*.

Boating on the Ciutadella lake

TOP 10 Performing Arts and Music Venues

Palau de la Música Catalana

1 Palau de la Música Catalana

Domenèch i Montaner's *Modernista* gem regularly serves up the best in jazz and classical music. It has lost some of its prestige to L'Auditori, but it still hosts some performances for Barcelona's Guitar Festival and attracts visiting musicians (see pp32–3).

2 El Molino

Vila i Vila 99 (Av Paral·lel) ▪ 93 396 71 91 ▪ Adm ▪ www.elmolinobcn.com

El Molino has been a musical theatre-bar since 1907. It hosts live music, cabaret shows, flamenco and tango performances. Book through the website.

3 Teatre Grec

The most atmospheric and magical of all Barcelona's venues, this open-air amphitheatre, set in thick, verdant forest, makes an incredible setting for ballet, music or theatre. Originally a quarry, it was converted in 1929 in preparation for the International Exhibition. It is open daily except during the summertime El Grec arts festival (see p96).

4 L'Auditori

MAP G1 ▪ C/Lepant 150 ▪ 93 247 93 00 ▪ DA

Located near the Teatre Nacional, this large auditorium is home to the Orquestra Simfònica de Barcelona and also houses the Museum of Music. Acoustics and visibility are excellent. In addition to classical music, it hosts regular jazz concerts.

5 Gran Teatre del Liceu

MAP L4 ▪ La Rambla ▪ 93 485 99 00 ▪ Guided tours in English available Mon–Fri, times vary ▪ Adm

Phoenix-like, the Liceu has risen from the ashes of two devastating fires since its inauguration in 1847 (see p16). Now one of the greatest opera houses in Europe, it is known for sterling performances by home-grown talent including one of the famed "three tenors", José Carreras.

Gran Teatre del Liceu

6 Harlem Jazz Club

The legendary Harlem Jazz Club in the Barrí Gòtic is one of the long-est surviving jazz and blues clubs in Barcelona. As well as offering great artistes, the admission charge usually includes a drink, and some shows are free (see p83).

Saxophonist at the Harlem Jazz Club

7 Mercat de les Flors
MAP B4 ▪ C/Lleida 59 ▪ 93 426
18 75 ▪ www.mercatflors.cat

The venue of choice for dance and performance theatre groups such as La Fura dels Baus and Comedians, whose incredible mixture of circus and drama is easily accessible to non-Catalan speakers.

8 Sala Apolo
MAP K4 ▪ C/Nou de la
Rambla 113 ▪ 93 441 40 01
▪ www.sala-apolo.com

An old dance hall with velvet-covered balconies and panelled bars, this place has reinvented itself as one of Barcelona's leading nightclubs. It attracts the latest in live techno and dance music (see p58).

9 Razzmatazz
This is one of the city's most famous venues. Hosting concerts several nights a week, the club's five areas offer a wide range of musical styles (see p104).

Gig at the Razzmatazz club

10 JazzSí Club – Taller de Musics
MAP J2 ▪ Requesens 2 ▪ 93 329 00 20
▪ Adm ▪ www.tallerdemusics.com/
jazzsi-club

Connected to the local music school, the JazzSí Club offers music workshops, lessons and daily concerts. Jazz, Cuban, flamenco or rock performances take place in the small, split-level venue between 7:30 (6:30 on Sun) and 9pm. Dinner is available from Monday to Friday.

TOP 10 VERSIÓN ORIGINAL CINEMAS AND FESTIVALS

Interior of the Filmoteca cinema

1 Filmoteca
C/Salvador Seguí 1–9 ▪ 93 567 10 70
▪ www.filmoteca.cat
Catalan government's repertory cinema screening three VO shows daily.

2 Verdi
MAP B2 ▪ C/Verdi 32 ▪ 93 238 79 90
▪ www.cines-verdi.com
An original VO cinema; five screens.

3 Icària Yelmo Cineplex
MAP H5 ▪ C/Salvador Espriu 61
▪ 90 222 09 22 ▪ www.yelmocines.es
Fifteen screens showing VO films.

4 Festival de Cine Documental Musical In-Edit
www.in-edit.org
This festival celebrates music and film.

5 Festival Internacional de Cinema Fantàstic de Catalunya
Sitges ▪ sitgesfilmfestival.com
Original version fantasy film festival.

6 Méliès Cinemes
MAP J1 ▪ C/Villarroel 102 ▪ 93 451 00 51 ▪ www.meliescinemes.com
Two-screen repertory cinema.

7 Cinemas Texas
MAP F1 ▪ C/Bailen 205 ▪ 93 348 47 70 ▪ www.cinemastexas.cat
Modern cinema showing VO films.

8 Sala Phenomena Experience
MAP G1 ▪ C/Sant Antoni Maria Claret 168 ▪ 93 252 77 43 ▪ www.phenomena-experience.com
State-of-the-art cinema for VO films.

9 Renoir Floridablanca
MAP C3 ▪ C/Floridablanca 135
▪ 93 228 93 93
A multiplex showing international films.

10 Sala Montjuïc
MAP B6 ▪ www.salamontjuic.org
This outdoor cinema near the castle shows cult films in summer.

🔟 Nightclubs and Bars

Evocative interior of Marsella

1 Marsella
Founded in 1820, this atmospheric throwback, run by the fifth generation of the Lamiel family, sits in the heart of the Barri Xinès area in El Raval. Marsella is one of the few places in town where you can enjoy *absenta* (absinthe). Settle in at one of the wrought-iron *Modernista* tables, surrounded by ancient mirrors and old religious statues, and test your mettle with the potent yellow liquor that is specially bottled for the bar *(see p92)*.

2 Sidecar Factory Club
Since 1982 this basement club has been the underground temple for rock, punk, indie and experimental music, hosting live shows and DJ sessions every night except Sunday. The bar at street level has outside seating. It is located in the popular Plaça Reial, which is one of the most interesting spots for nightlife *(see p83)*.

3 Otto Zutz
A sophisticated Barcelona nightlife institution, this three-storey disco is on the itinerary for well-heeled media types. The music verges on the mainstream with big-name DJs spinning everything from techno and hip-hop to current pop favourites *(see p122)*.

4 Jamboree
Venture underground – quite literally – to this popular, hopping jazz club-cum-nightclub in a vaulted space beneath Plaça Reial. Nightly live jazz sessions kick off at 8pm and 10pm. DJs take over later with dance sounds *(see p83)*.

5 Macarena Club

MAP L5 ■ C/Nou de Sant Francesc 5 ■ Open from midnight every night ■ www.macarenaclub.com
This minuscule but hugely popular club is located down a narrow street off the Plaça Reial. It features the best local and international DJs playing the latest dance and electronica for a lively crowd.

Performer at Sala Apolo

6 Sala Apolo
A converted theatre, now home to one of the city's best live music and club venues. The Nasty Mondays and Nitsa club nights are veritable institutions. Check the website for up-to-date programme information *(see p55)*.

***Previous pages** The flowing lines of Gaudí's remarkable Casa Batlló*

300 metres

7 La Terrrazza

MAP A3 ▪ Poble Espanyol ▪ Open Thu, Fri and Sat in summer, usually from midnight (times vary) ▪ www.laterrrazza.com ▪ Adm

Located inside the Poble Espanyol (see p97), La Terrrazza is one of the most popular summer nightclubs in Barcelona. The patio becomes the dance floor, the porches are bars and the garden provides a wonderfully refreshing chill-out area.

8 Café del Mar

C/De la Pau 12 ▪ Open daily ▪ www.cafedelmarclub barcelona.com

The Ibizan Café del Mar brand has opened this spectacular café, restaurant and club right on the seafront in the Forum area. It is already a favourite with Barcelona's fashionable crowd and its club nights are some of the hottest in the city.

9 Milano

Be careful not to miss it: stairs that are hidden from the street take you down to an elegant world of red velvet sofas, occasional live jazz and barmen who are experts in making cocktails. This is a den for good conversation rather than a crowded and noisy environment, and it's a popular gathering place for writers and journalists. The menu of snacks and drinks should please all tastes, but make sure you sample their Bloody Mary (see p111).

10 Razzmatazz

This is nothing less than the city's best all-round nightlife venue. Bands from around the world have played at Razzmatazz, including the Arctic Monkeys, Antony and the Johnsons, and Róisín Murphy. On Friday and Saturday nights (1–6am), the venue is divided into five clubs, each with its own distinct individual theme. The club also regularly hosts international guest DJs including big names such as Jarvis Cocker, Shaun Rider and Peter Smith among others (see p104).

Razzmatazz, one of Barcelona's top nightlife venues

🔟 Gay and Lesbian Hang-Outs

Partygoers at a Barcelona nightclub

1 Antinous Librería-Café
MAP D3 ■ C/Casanova 72
■ Closed Sun

Antinous is a popular gay meeting place in Barcelona's 'Gaixample' district. The café incorporates a spacious shop, stocking gifts, books and videos, and has a small bar area with exhibitions. Pick up a copy of *Gay Barcelona*, a free magazine available at most gay venues which gives the lowdown on the local scene.

2 Átame
MAP D3 ■ C/Consell de Cent 257
Átame takes its name from Almodóvar's film of the same title (*Tie Me Up! Tie Me Down!*) and has the same crazy, camp atmosphere. Open daily from 6pm for chill-out drinks, it gets packed at night, with a young crowd. Occasional drag queen shows.

3 Sauna Casanova
MAP D3 ■ C/Casanova 57 ■ Adm
This spotless gay sauna (for men only), has Turkish baths and Jacuzzis, as well as a handy bar and internet service. There are also private cabins, some with TV and DVDs.

4 Sala Diana
MAP E3 ■ C/Diputació 233
■ Closed Sun–Wed
This is the most popular lesbian club in Barcelona, although men are also welcome. It opens from 11pm to 3am and as it's not a big space, it's usually crowded. Music here focuses on favourites from the 70s, 80s, 90s and pop hits. On Thursdays there are burlesque dancers.

5 Metro
MAP J1 ■ C/Sepúlveda 185
■ Adm
The very popular, predominantly men-only Metro has two dance floors, one playing house, while the other has a more pop-orientated music policy and a pool table. The club really starts to liven up around 2am.

Metro club logo

6 El Cangrejo
MAP K5
■ C/Montserrat 9
■ Closed Sun–Wed
A historical venue, El Cangrejo ("The Crab") is a popular and very lively kitsch gay bar in the Raval quarter. Small and smoky, it is renowned for its Spanish 80s nights and its drag shows (from 11:30pm at weekends). Dance sessions last until 3am.

The popular kitsch gay bar El Cangrejo

7 Arena Madre
MAP E3 ■ C/Balmes 32
■ Open midnight–5am, 6am Sat
& Sun ■ Adm

A popular gay disco with a vibrant atmosphere and live performances ranging from cheeky stripteases to drag shows. The dance floor gets packed with a fun-loving crowd enjoying electronic and house music. There is also a dark room.

8 Sky Bar
MAP D2 ■ C/Aribau 33 ■ 93
323 93 93 ■ www.axelhotels.com

The rooftop terrace of the luxury Axel Hotel in the heart of the so-called "Gaixample" is a glamorous spot for vodka cocktails and poolside lounging, day and night. There are DJs and themed nights in summer. Reserve day beds in advance.

9 Punto BCN
MAP D3 ■ C/Muntaner 63

This relaxed, friendly bar has stayed in vogue for many years despite a fickle gay scene. It gets impossibly busy around midnight at weekends and the music is loud, but it's a good place to get fired up for a night out and get the latest on what's happening around town.

Crowds at popular Mar Bella beach

10 Beaches
MAP E6

In summer, gay men gather for some sun, fun and plenty of posing in front of the Club de Natació Barcelona on Barceloneta beach, near Plaça del Mar; the Mar Bella beach is also a popular hang-out.

TOP 10 GAY HOTSPOTS IN SITGES

Sitges bar

1 XXL
C/Joan Tarrida 7
Popular with the in-crowd, with a good drinks selection and techno music.

2 Parrots
Pl Industria 2
A Sitges classic, this bar has drag queen waiters and a lovely outdoor terrace.

3 El Horno
C/Joan Tarrida 6
Long-established gay bar, popular for drinks in the early evening.

4 Platja de l'Home Mort
The cliff path runs south to this intimate and gay-friendly cove. It has a fantastic beach bar, which is open in the summer.

5 Organic
C/Bonaire 12 ■ Adm
Organic is a gay-scene hotspot, popular with the fashion-industry crowd.

6 Beaches
The beach in front of Hotel Calípolis is a gay magnet, as is the nudist beach on the way to the town of Vilanova.

7 Night-time Cruising
The pier just past Hotel Calípolis is one of the busiest cruising spots. Prime time is between 3am and dawn.

8 Carousel
C/Joan Tarrida 14
A terrace bar great for soaking up the street life, with delicious cocktails and occasional shows.

9 Privilege
C/de Bonaire 24
One of the best gay music bars in town, with a different theme every night.

10 El Hotel Romàntic
C/St Isidre 33 ■ 93 894 83 75
A simple, gay-friendly hotel with a pretty garden.

🔟 Restaurants and Tapas Bars

The unpretentious interior of La Taverna del Clínic

1 La Taverna del Clínic

Slightly off the beaten track, this ordinary-looking tavern offers inventive (though pricey) tapas, accompanied by a great array of wines. Arrive early or be prepared to wait for a table (see p113).

2 Igueldo

Basque cuisine, prepared with flair and originality, is served here in elegant surroundings. Dishes include pig's trotters stuffed with *morcilla* (black pudding) and dried peach purée, or *zamburiñas*, a small scallop from the Atlantic. There is also a tapas bar at the entrance (see p113).

3 El Asador d'Aranda

This palatial restaurant, perched high above the city on Tibidabo, is popular with business-people and dishes up the best in Castilian cuisine. Sizable starters include *pica pica*, a tasty array of sausages, peppers and hams. The restaurant's signature main dish is *lechazo* (young lamb), roasted in a wood-fired oven (see p123).

4 Kaiku

This unassuming beachfront restaurant makes what is possibly the best paella in the city. It is on the menu as *arròs del xef*, and is prepared with smoked rice and succulent shellfish. The desserts are great too. In the summer, book a table on the terrace and enjoy the views and sea breeze (see p105).

5 Windsor

The modern Catalan *haute cuisine* dishes served in this elegant restaurant are based on seasonal local produce. Tasting menus feature *suquet de rape* (monkfish stew) and suckling lamb (see p113).

The bar area at Windsor

Alkimia

MAP D3 ▪ Ronda de San Antoni 41 ▪ 93 207 61 15 ▪ Closed Sat, Sun & lunch in Aug ▪ €€

Jordi Vilà has won countless awards and a Michelin star for his innovative New Catalan cuisine, taking time-honoured dishes and giving them an artful twist. This restaurant inside the Cervecería Moritz offers a suitably spectacular setting.

⑦ Cinc Sentits

This elegant Michelin-starred restaurant is known for its inventive cuisine. The tasting menu by chef Jordi Artal can be paired with specially-chosen wines. The set-price lunch menu (Monday to Friday) is a bargain *(see p113)*.

⑧ Pez Vela

Pg del Mare Nostrum 19/21 ▪ 93 221 63 17 ▪ €€

Contemporary decor and fresh Mediterranean cuisine coupled with some of the best sea views in the city make this a great spot for a special meal. Pez Vela is located underneath the W Barcelona hotel *(see p143)*.

⑨ Tickets Bar

MAP C4 ▪ Av Paral·lel 164 ▪ Closed Tue–Fri lunch, Sun, Mon, Easter, 3 weeks in Aug (advance online reservation advised, or call 606 225 545 for last-minute availability) ▪ www.ticketsbar.es ▪ €€

Run by El Bulli's founders, this Michelin-starred place serves inventive tapas such as tuna belly with ham and caviar, and Manchego cheese ice cream with bacon, mustard and cucumber.

 Disfrutar

MAP D2 ▪ Carrer de Villarroel, 163 ▪ Closed Sun & Mon ▪ www.disfrutarbarcelona.com ▪ €€

Avant-garde cuisine prepared by former El Bulli chefs is served here. Unconventional dishes such as a *gazpacho* sandwich (sourdough with feta spread and raw vegetables) or Moroccan style pigeon are on offer in a relaxed and modern setting.

TOP 10 TAPAS

Calamars a la Romana

1 Calamars
A savoury seafood option is *calamars a la romana* (deep-fried battered squid) or *calamars a la planxa* (grilled squid).

2 Patates Braves
This traditional tapas favourite consists of fried potatoes topped with a spicy sauce. Equally tasty are *patates* heaped with aioli (garlic and olive oil sauce).

3 Pa amb Tomàquet
A key part of any traditional tapas spread is this bread topped with tomato and olive oil.

4 Croquetes
These tasty fried morsels, usually paired with cod, ham or chicken in a béchamel sauce, are a perennial favourite.

5 Musclos o Escopinyes
Sample Barcelona's fruits of the sea with tapas of tasty mussels or cockles.

6 Truita de Patates
The most common tapas dish is this thick potato omelette, often topped with aioli (*allioli* in Catalan).

7 Ensaladilla Russa
"Russian salad" includes potatoes, onions, tuna (and often peas, carrots and other vegetables) all generously enveloped in mayonnaise.

8 Gambes a l'allet
An appetizing dish of prawns (shrimp) fried in garlic and olive oil.

9 Pernil Serrà
Cured ham is a Spanish obsession. The best, and most expensive, is Extremadura's speciality, Jabugo.

10 Fuet
Embotits (Catalan sausages) include the ever-popular *fuet*, a dry, flavourful variety most famously produced in the Catalonian town of Vic.

For a key to restaurant price ranges see p85

Cafés and Light Bites

1 Café Bliss

Hidden down a tiny side street in one of the loveliest Gothic squares in the old city is the delightful Café Bliss. There is a bright terrace, comfortable, inviting sofas and a range of international magazines and newspapers to browse through. It is perfect for coffee, cakes, light meals or a romantic drink in the evening (see p84).

2 Café de l'Òpera

MAP L4 ■ La Rambla 74

Kick back at this elegant late 19th-century café while being tended to by vested *cambrers* (waiters). This former *xocolateria* (confectionery café) – named after the Liceu opera house opposite – still serves fine gooey delights such as *xurros amb xocolata* (strips of fried dough with thick chocolate). It's perfect for people-watching on La Rambla.

Café de l'Òpera on La Rambla

The smart interior of Bar Lobo

3 Bar Lobo

MAP Q4 ■ C/Pintor Fortuny 3
■ 93 481 53 46 ■ Open daily until midnight

This chic café is a popular brunch spot during the day, but it really comes alive in the evenings. From Thursday to Saturday it opens until 2:30am for drinks. The terrace is very popular.

4 Laie Llibreria Cafè

Tuck into a generous buffet of rice, pasta, greens, chicken and more at this charming, long-running Eixample café-bookshop. You can also opt for the well-priced vegetarian menu, which includes soup, salad and a main dish (see p112).

5 Federal Café

MAP D4 ■ C/Parlament 39
■ 93 187 36 07 ■ Closed Sun evenings

The airy Federal Café is a local hipster hang-out serving amazing coffee, brunch and light meals, as well as cocktails in the evening. There is a romantic little roof terrace, free Wi-Fi and English-language magazines to flick through.

6 Bar Kasparo

MAP L2 ■ Pl Vicenç Martorell 4
■ Closed Mon and Sun

This laid-back outdoor café serves a varied menu of fresh international fare with an Asiatic twist, such as chicken curry and Greek salad. After the sun dips beneath the horizon, a bar-like vibe takes over, fuelled by beer and cider.

7 Alsur Café
MAP F3 ■ C/Roger de Llúria 23
■ 93 624 15 77

Its nonstop kitchen serves brunch, tapas, homemade cakes, sandwiches and salads. Free Wi-Fi, big windows and a warm atmosphere make it the perfect place to work or read the newspaper. There's also a branch in El Born district and in front of the Palau de la Música.

8 En Aparté
A light-filled café serving a good selection of French cheeses and cold meats accompanied by French wines. The crème brûlée is a must and the fixed price lunch menu is good value. There are tables outside overlooking the square *(see p84)*.

9 Granja Dulcinea
MAP L3 ■ C/Petritxol 2
■ Closes at 9pm

The *xocolateries* and *granjes* on Carrer Petritxol *(see p80)* have been satiating sugar cravings for decades. Among them is this old-fashioned café with to-die-for delights from *xurros amb xocolata* to strawberries and whipped cream. In summer, *orxates* and *granissats* are on the menu.

Pastries at Granja Dulcinea

10 La Tartela
MAP B3
■ C/Llança 32 ■ 93 105 10 15

A pretty little spot just off the Plaça Espanya, serving cakes, quiches, lasagna and outstanding coffee. It has a few pavement tables and great service.

TOP 10 CAFÉ DRINKS

A cup of strong *cigaló*

1 Cigaló
For coffee with a bite, try a *cigaló* (*carajillo*), which has a shot of either *conyac* (cognac), *whisky* or *ron* (rum).

2 Tallat and Cafè Sol
A *tallat* is a small cup of coffee with a dash of milk. A *cafè sol* is just plain coffee. In the summer, opt for either one *amb gel* (with ice).

3 Cafè amb llet
Traditionally enjoyed in the morning, *cafè amb llet* is a large milky coffee.

4 Orxata
This sweet, milky-white drink made from the tiger nut is a local summer time favourite.

5 Granissat
Slake your thirst with a cool *granissat*, a crushed-ice drink that is usually lemon-flavoured.

6 Aigua
Stay hydrated with *aigua mineral* (mineral water) – *amb gas* is sparkling, *sense gas*, still.

7 Cacaolat
A chocolate-milk concoction, which is one of Spain's most popular sweet drink exports.

8 Una Canya and Una Clara
Una canya is roughly a quarter litre of *cervesa de barril* (draught beer). *Una clara* is the same size but made up of equal parts beer and fizzy lemonade.

9 Cava
Catalonia's answer to champagne is its home-grown *cava* – Freixenet and Codorníu are the most famous brands.

10 Sangría
This ever-popular concoction of red wine, fruit juices and spirits is ordered at cafés throughout the city.

Best Shopping Areas

② Carrer Girona
MAP P1

Those looking for fashion bargains should head to Carrer Girona (metro Tetuan), which is lined with designer and high-street outlet stores. Most offer women's fashions including streetwear from brands such as Mango, evening wear and shoes from Catalan designers Etxart & Panno, and upmarket designs from the likes of Javier Simorra.

③ Plaça de Catalunya and Carrer Pelai
MAP L/M1 ■ El Corte Inglés: Pl de Catalunya 14 ■ Open 9:30am–9:30pm Mon–Sat ■ El Triangle: C/Pelai 39 ■ Open 10am–10pm Mon–Sat

The city's bustling centrepiece is also its commercial crossroads, flanked by the department store El Corte Inglés and the shopping mall El Triangle, which includes FNAC (books, CDs, videos) and Séphora (perfumes and cosmetics). Lined with shoe and clothing shops, the nearby Carrer Pelai is said to have more pedestrian traffic than any other shopping street in Spain.

④ Rambla de Catalunya
MAP E2

The genteel, classier extension of La Rambla, this well-maintained street offers a refreshing change from its cousin's more downmarket carnival

① Passeig de Gràcia
MAP E3

Right in the heart of the city, Barcelona's grand avenue of lavish *Modernista* buildings is fittingly home to the city's premier fashion and design stores. From the international big league (Chanel, Gucci, Stella McCartney) to Spain's heavy hitters (Camper, Loewe, Zara, Mango), it's all here. The wide boulevards either side reveal more designer shopping, notably Carrer Consell de Cent, which is also dotted with art galleries, and Carrers Mallorca, València and Roselló.

Top design and fashion stores on Passeig de Gràcia

The chic Rambla de Catalunya

atmosphere. Chic shops and cafés, as well as their moneyed customers, pepper the street's length from Plaça de Catalunya to Diagonal. Here you'll find everything from fine footwear and leather bags to linens and lamps (see p109).

5 Portal de l'Àngel
MAP M2

Once a Roman thoroughfare leading into the walled city of Barcino, today the pedestrian street of Portal de l'Àngel is traversed by hordes of shoppers toting bulging bags. The street is chock-full of shoe, clothing, jewellery and accessory shops.

6 Maremagnum
MAP N5 ■ Muelle de España 5 ■ Open 10am–10pm daily

This shopping centre on the water's edge is open every day of the year. All of the main clothing chains can be found here, along with a good variety of cafés and restaurants.

7 Carrer Portaferrissa
MAP M3

From zebra platform shoes to bellybutton rings and pastel baby T-shirts, this street's other name could well be Carrer "Trendy". In addition to all the usual high-street chains – from H&M to Mango and NafNaf – along this strip you'll find El Mercadillo, crammed with hip little shops selling spiked belts, frameless sunglasses, surf wear and the like. After stocking up on

fashion, stop for a box of prettily-wrapped chocolates at Fargas on nearby Carrer del Pi (No. 16).

8 Gràcia
MAP F1

Old bookstores, family-run grocery stores and independent boutiques selling trendy, often vintage, fashion, homewares and accessories cluster along Carrer Astúries (and its side streets) and along Travessera de Gràcia. A string of contemporary clothing and shoe shops also line Gran de Gràcia.

9 El Born
MAP P4

Amid El Born's web of streets are all sorts of art and design shops. Passeig del Born and Carrer Rec are dotted with innovative little galleries (from sculpture to interior design), plus clothing and shoe boutiques. The best area for original fashion and accessories (see p78).

Handbag store, Avinguda Diagonal

10 Avinguda Diagonal
MAP D1

Big and brash, the traffic-choked Avinguda Diagonal is hard to miss – a cacophonous avenue that cuts diagonally across the entire city. It is a premier shopping street, particularly west of Passeig de Gràcia to its culmination in L'Illa mall and the large El Corte Inglés department store near Plaça Maria Cristina. Lining this long stretch is a host of high-end clothing and shoe stores – including Armani, Loewe and Hugo Boss – as well as interior design shops, jewellery and watch purveyors, and more.

TOP 10 Most Fascinating Markets

① Mercat de la Boqueria
MAP L3 ■ La Rambla 91
■ Open 8am–8pm Mon–Sat

The most famous food market in Barcelona is conveniently located on La Rambla (see pp16–17). Freshness reigns supreme and shoppers are spoiled for choice, with hundreds of stalls selling everything from vine-ripened tomatoes to haunches of beef and wedges of Manchego cheese. The city's seaside status is in full evidence at the fish stalls.

② Fira de Santa Llúcia
MAP N3 ■ Pl de la Seu
■ Open 1–23 Dec: 10am–8pm (times may vary) daily

The Christmas season is officially under way when local artisans set up shop outside the cathedral for the annual Christmas fair. Well worth a visit, if only to peruse the row upon row of *caganers*, miniature figures squatting to *fer caca* (take a poop). Uniquely Catalan, the *caganers* are usually hidden at the back of nativity scenes. This unusual celebration of the scatological also appears in other Christmas traditions.

③ Els Encants
Trading beneath metal canopies, Els Encants, east of the city, is one of Europe's oldest flea

Produce at Mercat de la Boqueria

markets, dating back to the 14th century. It sells everything from second-hand clothes, electrical appliances and toys to used books. Discerning shoppers can fit out an entire kitchen from an array of pots and pans. Bargain-hunters should come early (see p108).

④ Book and Coin Market at Mercat de Sant Antoni
Map D2 ■ C/Comte d'Urgell
■ Open 8am–3pm Sun

For book lovers, there's no better way to spend Sunday morning than browsing at this market south of La Rambla. You'll find a mind-boggling assortment of weathered paperbacks, ancient tomes, stacks of old magazines, comics, postcards and lots more, from coins to videos.

⑤ Fira Artesana
MAP M3 ■ Pl del Pi ■ Open 10am–10pm first & third Fri, Sat & Sun of the month

The Plaça del Pi (see p47) brims with natural and organic foods during the Fira Artesana, when artisanal food producers bring their goods to this corner of the Barri Gòtic. The market specializes in homemade cheeses and honey – from clear clover honey from the Pyrenees to nutty concoctions from Morella.

Stalls at Els Encants flea market

⑥ Fira de Filatelia i Numismàtica

MAP L4 ▪ Pl Reial ▪ Open 9am–2:30pm Sun

Arranged around the elegant Plaça Reial (see p78), this popular stamp and coin market draws avid collectors from all over the city. The newest collectors' items are phone cards and old *xapes de cava* (cava bottle cork foils). When the market ends – and the local police go to lunch – a makeshift flea market takes over. Old folks and immigrants from the *barri* haul out their belongings – old lamps, clothing, junk – and lay it all out for sale on cloths on the ground.

⑦ Mercat de Barceloneta

MAP F6 ▪ Pl Font 1, Barceloneta ▪ Open 7am–3pm Mon–Thu & Sat, 7am–8pm Fri

The striking Barceloneta market overlooks an expansive square. In addition to colourful produce stalls, there is a good selection of bars and bakeries here.

⑧ Mercat dels Antiquaris

MAP N3 ▪ Pl de la Seu ▪ Open 10am–9pm Thu (except Aug)

Antiques aficionados and collectors contentedly rummage through jewellery, watches, candelabras, embroidery and bric-a-brac at this long-running antiques market in front of the cathedral.

⑨ Mercat del Art de la Plaça de Sant Josep Oriol

MAP M4 ▪ Pl de Sant Josep Oriol ▪ Open 11am–8:30pm Sat, 10am–3pm Sun

At weekends, local artists flock to this Barri Gòtic square to set up their easels and sell their art. You'll find a range including watercolours of Catalan landscapes to oil paintings of churches and castles.

⑩ Mercat de Santa Caterina

MAP N3 ▪ Av Francesc Cambó 16 ▪ Open 7:30am–2pm Mon, 7:30am–3:30pm Tue, Wed & Sat, 7:30am–8:30pm Thu & Fri

Each *barri* has its own food market with tempting displays but this one boasts a spectacular setting. The building was designed by Catalan architect Enric Miralles (1995–2000).

The striking Mercat de Santa Caterina

Barcelona for Free

Relaxing on a Barcelona beach

1 Beaches

Barcelona boasts 10 beaches, stretching for over 4.5 km (3 miles) along the coast. Between Easter and October they are dotted with *xiringuitos* selling drinks and snacks, and have lifeguards, sun lounger rental and even a beach library.

2 Sunday Afternoons at City Museums

www.bcn.cat/museus/
diumengestarda

All city-run museums are free at least one afternoon a month, usually the first Saturday or Sunday of the month, and several, including the Museu de Catalunya, Museu del Disseny, Centre de Cultura Contemporánea de Barcelona (CCCB), Museu de la Història de Barcelona (MUHBA) and Museu Blau (main site of the Museu de Ciències Naturals), are free Sunday afternoon from 3pm. A full list of these can be found on the Barcelona Turisme website.

3 Font Màgica

The Magic Fountain thrills with its wonderful sound and light shows, a balletic synchronicity of light and water. Multicoloured jets of water leap to different soundtracks and soar in elegant rows all the way up to MNAC on the hill behind. The programme, ranging from classical to Disney tunes, is on the Barcelona Turisme website. The Piromusical, a huge firework, music and laser show that is Festes de la Mercè's closing event, also takes place here *(see p95)*.

4 Música als Parcs

City parks host free summer concerts during the annual Música als Parcs programme. Musicians from around the world perform jazz, classical and contemporary music. The Parc de la Ciutadella is the main venue, but several other parks are involved. Check the Barcelona Turisme website for full listings.

5 La Capella

MAP K3 ■ C/Hospital 56
■ Opening times vary, check website
■ lacapella.bcn.cat

The chapel at the Antic Hospital de la Santa Creu *(see p89)* has been converted into a fantastic art space hosting exhibitions of contemporary works by up-and-coming artists. It offers free guided tours in Spanish and Catalan at 6pm on Saturdays.

6 Festes

Every neighbourhood has its own *festa major* (various dates, Jun–Sep), ranging from the bacchanalian romp in Gràcia to the more modest celebrations of Poble Sec. You'll see various Catalan traditions, from *castells* (human towers) to *correfocs* (fire-running) – and all for free. One of the biggest festivals is the Festes de la Mercè *(see p72)*.

Fireworks at the Festes de la Mercè

7 Jardí Botànic Històric
MAP A4 ■ Av dels Muntanyans ■ Open 10am–6pm daily (to 7pm in summer) ■ Adm ■ museuciencies.cat

The wonderful Historic Botanic Gardens, hidden away down a gully behind the Museu Nacional d'Art de Catalunya, are well worth the effort of seeking out. The pretty winding paths, shaded by centuries-old trees, are an excellent place for escaping the summer heat.

8 Carretera de les Aigües
Running along the side of the Collserola park (see p119), this path is popular with mountain-bikers, runners and walkers, and offers spectacular views across the city and out to sea. Getting there is fun too: take the FGC train to Peu de la Funicular, then ride the funicular halfway up, to the *carretera* stop.

Miró mosaic, Boqueria Market

9 Street Art
The streets are filled with art by world-famous artists including Botero's *Cat* on the Rambla del Raval; Lichtenstein's *Head of Barcelona* and Mariscal's *Gambrinus* at the port; Gehry's glittering *Fish* by the sea; and Miró's *Woman and Bird* in the Parc de Joan Miró (see p49) and mosaic at the Mercat de la Boqueria (see p68).

10 Open House Barcelona
www.48hopenhousebarcelona.org
Peek into private homes, exciting new buildings and historic monuments during the city's annual Open House weekend. Many buildings not usually open to the public can be visited, including the Arc de Triomf and the Ateneu cultural centre.

TOP 10 MONEY-SAVING TIPS

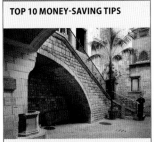

Entrance to the Museu Picasso

1 The best travel option is the T-10, a multiperson travel card valid for 10 journeys in zones 1 to 6 and the airport train.

2 If you know you're going to be visiting a lot of museums and using the public transport system, invest in the Barcelona Card, which starts at €20 for 48 hours.

3 The Art Ticket, which allows entry to six major art museums for €30 is an excellent deal for culture buffs.

4 Many nightclubs offer free entry if you arrive early (before midnight).

5 Several theatres and cinemas offer reduced prices on *Dia del Espectador*, usually Monday, Tuesday or Wednesday, or for the day's first performance (usually around 4pm).

6 At weekday lunchtimes, many restaurants serve a good-value *menú del migdia* with two or three courses, a glass of wine and perhaps a coffee.

7 Pack a picnic of tasty local produce and head to the Montjuïc parks (the Parc Jacint Mossen Cinto with its lily ponds and shady nooks is a particular favourite) or to the beaches to dine for a fraction of the price of a restaurant.

8 Some university residences, such as the Residència Àgora BCN and the Residència Erasmus, offer cheap beds during the summer break.

9 For fashion bargains, hit the outlet stores on Carrer Girona, near the Gran Via. Brands include Mango, Etxart & Panno and Nice Things.

10 All products offered by Barcelona's tourist service, from the Bus Turístic to walking tours, are sold at a discount (usually 10 percent) in their online shop.

Catalan Folk Festivals and Traditions

Gegants, **Festes de la Mercè**

1 Festes de la Mercè
Week of 23 Sep

Barcelona's main festival is a riotous week-long celebration in honour of La Mercè *(see p41)*. The night sky lights up with fireworks, outdoor concerts are held, and there's barely a bottle of *cava* left in the city by the festival's end. Parades and processions feature *gegants* – giant wooden puppets operated by people.

2 El Dia de Sant Jordi
23 Apr

On this spring day, Barcelona is transformed into a vibrant open-air book and flower market. Men and women exchange presents of roses, to celebrate Sant Jordi *(see p41)*, and books, in tribute to Cervantes and Shakespeare, who both died on 23 April 1616.

3 La Revetlla de Sant Joan
23 Jun

In celebration of St John and the start of summer, this is Catalonians' night to play with fire – and play they do, with gusto. Fireworks streak through the night sky and bonfires are set ablaze on beaches and in towns throughout the region.

4 Festes de Sant Medir
Around 3 Mar

A 10th-century hermitage is the focus of a picturesque pilgrimage featuring carriages and costumed attendants on horseback. Sweets are thrown from the carriages, which is a treat for the kids.

5 Carnaval in Sitges
3–4 days Feb

The buzzing beach town of Sitges *(see p127)* explodes during Carnaval, celebrated in flamboyant fashion. Over-the-top floats carry drag queens, there are lip-synching contests and a fresh-off-the-beach crowd warmed by sun and plenty of beer.

6 Festa de la Patum
Corpus Christi (May)

The village of Berga (90 km/60 miles north of Barcelona) hosts one of Catalonia's liveliest festivals. The event gets its name from the folks who used to chant *patum* (the sound of a drum). Streets spill over with merrymakers as fireworks crackle and dwarfs, devils and dragons dance atop parade floats.

7 Festa Major de Gràcia
Mid- to late Aug

During this week-long *festa*, the largest party of the summer, revellers congregate in Gràcia's decorated streets. Parades, open-air concerts, fireworks and plentiful supplies of beer and *cava* fuel the infectious merriment.

Festa Major de Gràcia celebrations

8 Castells
Jun

Castells is one of Catalonia's most spectacular folk traditions. Trained *castellers* stand on each others' shoulders using precise techniques to create a human castle – the highest tower takes the prize. The crowning moment is when a child scales the human mass to make the sign of the cross. *Castells* are often performed in Plaça Sant Jaume.

Castellers building a human tower

9 Sardanes

"The magnificent, moving ring" is how Catalan poet Joan Maragall described the *sardana*, Catalonia's regional dance. Subdued yet intricate, it is performed to the tunes of the *cobla*, a traditional brass and woodwind band. *Sardanes* can be seen in Plaça de la Seu and Plaça Sant Jaume year round (see p19).

10 Catalan Christmas and Cavalcada de Reis

The *Nadal* (Christmas) season begins on 1 December with the arrival of the festive artisan fairs. On 5 January is the Cavalcada de Reis, the spectacular Parade of the Three Kings. In Barcelona, the kings arrive by sea and are welcomed by city officials in front of transfixed children.

TOP 10 MUSIC, THEATRE AND ART FESTIVALS

Revellers at the Festival del Sónar

1 Festival del Sónar
Mid-Jun ▪ www.sonar.es
This electronic music and multimedia festival is an explosion of music and the latest in audiovisual production.

2 Grec Festival Barcelona
Late Jun–Jul ▪ 93 316 10 00 ▪ www.lameva.barcelona.cat/grec
Barcelona's largest music, theatre and dance festival.

3 Festival Internacional de Jazz
Oct–Nov ▪ 93 481 70 40 ▪ www.jazz.barcelona
Big-name and experimental live jazz.

4 Festival Internacional de Cinema Fantàstic de Catalunya
Early Oct ▪ sitgesfilmfestival.com
The world's best fantasy film festival.

5 Festival de Música Antiga
Sep–Jul ▪ www.auditori.cat
Concerts of early music in the Barri Gòtic and L'Auditori.

6 Música als Parcs
Jun–Aug ▪ www.facebook.com/MusicaParcs
Classical music and jazz concerts are held in the city's parks.

7 Guitar BCN
Feb–Jun ▪ 93 481 70 40 ▪ www.theproject.es
International guitar festival.

8 L'Alternativa Film Festival
Nov ▪ www.alternativa.cccb.org
Showcases the best independent films.

9 Ciutat Flamenco
Late May ▪ 93 443 43 46 ▪ www.ciutatflamenco.com
A week of outstanding flamenco music at the Mercat de les Flors.

10 Primavera Sound
Late May ▪ www.primaverasound.com
A pop, rock and underground dance music festival that features many big-name acts.

Barcelona
Area by Area

A view of Barcelona, with the
Sagrada Família in the background

🔟 Barri Gòtic and La Ribera

Starting as the Roman settlement of Barcino, the city grew over the years, culminating in a building boom in the 14th and 15th centuries. Barri Gòtic is a beautifully-preserved neighbourhood of Gothic buildings, squares and atmospheric alleys, with the cathedral at its religious and social heart a reminder of its medieval heyday. Extending east of Barri Gòtic is the ancient *barri* of La Ribera, with lovely Carrer Montcada and the Museu Picasso.

Mosaic, Palau de la Música Catalana

BARRI GÒTIC AND LA RIBERA

Barcelona Cathedral
Soaring over the Barri Gòtic is Barcelona's mighty cathedral, which dates from 1298 (see pp18–19).

2 Museu Picasso
Discover the youthful output of one of the most revered artists of the 20th century (see pp30–31).

3 Palau de la Música Catalana
The city's most prestigious concert hall is a breathtaking monument to both *la música Catalana* and the *Modernista* aesthetic (see pp22–3).

❶	**Top 10 Sights** see pp76–9
①	**Restaurants and Tapas Bars** see p85
①	**Shops** see p81
①	**Clubs and Music Venues** see p83
①	**The Best of the Rest** see p80
①	**Cafés and Light Eats** see p84
①	**Cocktail and Conversation Spots** see p82

Façade of the Palau de la Generalitat

4 Plaça de Sant Jaume
MAP M4 ▪ Palau de la Generalitat: 012 (within the city); Open 10:30am–1:30pm second & fourth Sat & Sun of the month for guided tours, advance booking essential; www.president.cat/pres_gov/president/ca/presidencia/palau-generalitat/visites.html ▪ Ajuntament: Open 10am–1:30pm Sun for guided tours (English at 10am)

The site of the Plaça de Sant Jaume (see p46) was once the nucleus of Roman Barcino. With these roots, it seems fitting that the square is home to Barcelona's two most important government buildings: the Palau de la Generalitat (the seat of Catalonian parliament) and the Ajuntament (city hall). Look for the detailed carved relief of Sant Jordi, Catalonia's patron saint, on the 15th-century Generalitat façade. Within is the beautiful 1434 Capella de Sant Jordi (see p41). A highlight of the Gothic 15th-century Ajuntament is the Saló de Cent, from where the Council of One Hundred ruled the city from 1372 to 1714. Also of note is the Pati dels Tarongers, a lovely arcaded courtyard planted with orange trees and overlooked by interesting gargoyles.

EL BORN

If you're hankering for a proper martini or some alternative jazz, then look no further than El Born, a sleepy-turned-hip neighbourhood "reborn" several years ago. Students and artists moved in, attracted by cheap rents and airy warehouses, fostering an arty vibe that now blends in with the area's old-time aura. Experimental design shops share the narrow streets with traditional balconied buildings festooned with laundry hung out to dry. The buzzing Passeig de Born, lined with bars and cafés, leads onto the inviting Plaça Comercial, where the cavernous Born Market (in operation 1870–1970) has been converted into a cultural centre and exhibition space.

Three Graces fountain, Plaça Reial

designed by Gaudí in 1879, and at its centre is a wrought-iron fountain representing the Three Graces. The palm-lined square has a cluster of restaurants, bars and cafés that are constantly busy.

⑤ Museu d'Història de Barcelona (MUHBA)

MAP M4 ▪ Pl del Rei ▪ Open 10am–7pm Tue–Sat (to 8pm Sun) ▪ Adm; free first Sun of the month, every Sun after 3pm ▪ www.barcelona.cat/museuhistoria/en

The medieval Plaça del Rei (see p46) contains the core site of the Museu d'Història de Barcelona, encom-passing remains ranging from Roman Barcino to the Middle Ages. These include Casa Padellàs (see p42) and the Palau Reial, which contains the Capella de Santa Àgata (see p41) and the Saló del Tinell, a massive arched hall where Ferdinand and Isabel met Columbus after his 1492 voyage to the Americas. The museum also has one of the largest underground excavations of Roman ruins on display in Europe, including a 2nd-century laundry and dyeing workshop and 3rd-century garum factory and winery.

⑥ Plaça Reial

MAP L4

Late 19th-century elegance meets sangria-drinking café society in the arcaded Plaça Reial, one of the city's most entertaining squares (see p46). The *Modernista* lampposts were

⑦ Museu Frederic Marès

MAP N3 ▪ Pl de Sant Iu 5–6 ▪ Open 10am–7pm Tue–Sat, 11am–8pm Sun ▪ Adm; free first Sun of the month, every Sun after 3pm ▪ www.museumares.bcn.cat

This fascinating museum houses the collection of wealthy Catalan sculptor Frederic Marès. No mere hobby collector, the astute (and obsessive) Marès amassed holdings that a modern museum curator would die for. Among them is an array of religious icons and statues, dating from Roman times to the present, and the curious "Museu Sentimental", which displays everything from ancient watches to fans and dolls. Also worth a visit during summer is Cafè d'Estiu (see p84), a sunny spot for a break on the museum's patio.

Museu Frederic Marès

⑧ Església de Santa Maria del Mar

MAP P5 ▪ Pl de Santa Maria 1 ▪ Open 9am–1pm & 5–8:30pm Mon–Sat, 10am–2pm & 5–8pm Sun ▪ Guided tours 1:15pm (except Sat & Sun), 2pm, 3pm, 5:15pm daily ▪ Adm for guided tours (includes rooftop visit) ▪ www.santamariadelmarbarcelona.org

The spacious, breathtaking interior of this 14th-century church (see p40), designed by architect Berenguer de Montagut, is the city's premier example of the austere Catalan Gothic style. The church is dedicated to St Mary of the Sea, the patron saint of sailors, and an ancient model ship hangs near one of the statues of the Virgin. Dubbed "the people's church", this is a popular spot for exchanging wedding vows.

 Museu de Cultures del Món

MAP P4 ■ C/Montcada 14 ■ Open 10am–7pm Tue–Sat (to 8pm Sun) ■ Adm; free first Sun of the month, every Sun after 3pm ■ museucultures mon.bcn.cat/en

The Museum of World Cultures, in the 16th-century Nadal and Marqués de Lliò palaces, showcases the cultures of Asia, Africa, America and Oceania. Highlights include Hindu sculptures, Japanese paintings, Nazca ceramics, brass plaques from Benin and indigenous Australian art.

Exhibits, Museu de Cultures del Món

El Call

MAP M4 ■ Singagoga Major: C/ Marlet 2; 93 317 07 90; Adm ■ Centro d'Interpretació del Call: Plaçeta del Manuel Ribé s/n; 93 256 21 22; Adm

El Call was home to one of Spain's largest Jewish communities until their expulsion in the 15th century. Some original buildings have survived, although a small (now restored) synagogue, believed to be one of the oldest in Europe, is on Carrer de Marlet. There is also an interpretation centre dedicated to El Call, run by the city's history museum.

ROMAN BARCELONA

[map showing: Avinguda Portal de l'Àngel, Plaça de la Vila de Madrid, Barcelona Cathedral, Plaça del Rei, Café-Bar L'Antiquari, Plaça de Ramon Berenguer el Gran, Temple d'August, Museu d'Història de Barcelona, Plaça Sant Jaume, Jaume I metro station, Bliss, Pati Llimona]

► MORNING

Start at the Jaume I metro stop. Walk up Via Laietana to the **Plaça de Ramon Berenguer el Gran** (see p80), which is backed by an impressive stretch of Roman walls. Return to the metro and turn right onto C/Jaume I to get to the **Plaça Sant Jaume**, the site of the old Roman forum. Leading off to the left is C/Ciutat, which becomes C/Regomir: at No. 3 is **Pati Llimona** (see p80), with an extensive section of Roman walls, one of the four main gateways into the city and the ruins of some thermal baths. There's a good, inexpensive café at Pati Llimona, or you can enjoy a light lunch at **Bliss** (Plaça de Sant Just).

AFTERNOON

Return to the Plaça Sant Jaume and cross it into tiny C/Paradís, where you'll find vestiges of the **Temple d'August**, a MUHBA site. At the end of the street, turn right and make for the Plaça del Rei. Stop for coffee at the **Café-Bar L'Antiquari** (see p84) before visiting the **Museu d'Història de Barcelona** (MUHBA), where you can explore the remains of Roman Barcino. Walk back to C/Comtes, which flanks **Barcelona Cathedral**, turn right and cross Plaça Nova to C/Arcs, which leads to Avinguda Portal de l'Àngel. Turn left down C/Canuda to reach the **Plaça de la Vila de Madrid**, where several Roman sarcophagi, found outside the walls according to Roman tradition, are arranged along an old Roman road.

See map on pp76–7 ←

The Best of the Rest

Neo-Gothic bridge, Carrer del Bisbe

 Carrer del Bisbe
MAP M3

Medieval Carrer del Bisbe is flanked by the Gothic Cases dels Canonges (House of Canons) and the Palau de la Generalitat (see p77). Connecting the two is an eye-catching 1928 Neo-Gothic arched stone bridge.

2 Carrer de Santa Llúcia
MAP M3

At the weekend, amateur opera singers perform on this medieval street, home to the Casa de l'Ardiaca (see p19), which has a pretty little patio with palm trees and a fountain.

3 Capella de Sant Cristòfol
MAP M4 ▪ C/Regomir 6–8

This chapel dedicated to Sant Cristòfor, the patron saint of travellers, dates from 1503, although it was remodeled in the 1890s. Drivers bring their cars to the chapel annually on the saint's feast day (25 July) to be blessed.

4 Carrer Montcada
MAP P4

The "palace row" of La Ribera is lined with Gothic architectural gems, including the 15th-century Palau Aguilar, which is now home

to the Museu Picasso (see pp30–31), and the 17th-century Palau Dalmases with its Gothic chapel.

 Plaça de Ramon Berenguer el Gran
MAP N3

This square boasts one of the largest preserved sections of Barcelona's impressive Roman walls.

 Carrer Regomir and Carrer del Correu Vell
MAP M5

You'll find splendid Roman remains on Carrer Regomir, most notably within the medieval Pati Llimona. Two Roman towers can be seen on nearby Carrer del Correu Vell, and there are remnants of Roman walls on the Plaça Traginers.

7 Plaça de Sant Felip Neri
MAP M3

Sunlight filters through tall trees in this hidden oasis of calm. The plaça is home to the Museu del Calçat, which showcases footwear.

8 Carrer Petritxol
MAP L3

This well-maintained medieval street is lined with traditional granges and xocolateries (cafés and chocolate shops). The famous Sala Parés art gallery, which once exhibited Picasso, Casas and other Catalan contemporaries, is also found here.

9 Església de Sant Just i Sant Pastor
MAP M4

This Gothic church, completed in 1342, has sculptures dating back to the 9th century and 5th-century Visigothic baptismal fonts.

10 Església de Santa Anna
MAP M2

Mere paces from La Rambla is the unexpected tranquillity of this Romanesque church with its leafy 15th-century Gothic cloister.

Shops

 Escribà Confiteria i Fleca
MAP L3 ▪ La Rambla 83

If the glistening pastries and towering chocolate creations aren't enough of a lure, then the *Modernista* storefront certainly is. Buy goodies to go or enjoy them in the café.

 La Manual Alpargatera
MAP M4 ▪ C/Avinyó 7

What do Pope John Paul II, Jack Nicholson, Salvador Dalí, *sardana* dancers and legions of *Barcelonins* have in common? They all bought their *alpargatas* or exquisite handmade espadrilles and straw hats at this traditional shoe shop.

Shoes from La Manual Alpargatera

 Coquette
MAP P5 ▪ C/Rec 65

Divine women's accessories, fashions and toiletries can be found in this loft-style store. Among the labels stocked here are top Spanish and French names, such as Hoss, Intropia and See by Chloé.

4 **Sombreria Mil**
MAP N1 ▪ C/Fontanella 20

This traditional hat shop celebrated its centenary in 2017, and offers a fine range of headwear (including the traditional Catalan beret) for men and women.

 Beatriz Furest
MAP P5 ▪ C/Esparteria 1

Handcrafted, beautiful bags and purses by Barcelonin designer Beatriz Furest are on sale in this small, chic boutique.

6 **Casa Colomina**
MAP M3 ▪ C/Cucurulla 2

Sink your teeth into the Spanish nougat-and-almond speciality *torró*. Casa Colomina, established in 1908, offers a tantalizing array, including chocolate and marzipan varieties.

7 **Cereria Subirà**
MAP N4 ▪ Baixada Llibreteria 7

Founded in 1761, this is Barcelona's oldest shop, crammed with every kind of candle imaginable, from plain white to waxy works of art.

8 **Vila Viniteca**
C/Agullers 7

This is one of the city's best wine merchants stocking a range of wines and spirits. An adjoining shop sells quality Spanish delicacies, including hams, cheeses and olive oil.

9 **Guantería Alonso**
MAP M2 ▪ C/Santa Anna 27

This long-established shop is the place to visit for colourful hand-painted fans, handmade gloves, delicately embroidered mantillas and shawls, ornamental combs and other traditional Spanish accessories.

10 **L'Arca**
MAP M3 ▪ C/Banys Nous 20

Find amazing antique clothing from flapper dresses to boned corsets, silk shawls, puff-sleeved shirts and pin-tucked shirt fronts here. They special-ise in antique wedding dresses.

Vintage silk shawl at L'Arca

See map on pp76–7 →

Cocktail and Conversation Spots

1 Schilling
MAP M4 ■ C/Ferran 23

Fronted by large windows overlooking the throngs on Carrer Ferran, this spacious bar draws a sociable mix of visitors and locals.

2 Bar L'Ascensor
MAP M4 ■ C/Bellafila 3

An old-fashioned, dark-wood elevator – *ascensor* in Catalan and Spanish – serves as the entrance to this dimly lit, convivial bar frequented by a cocktail-swilling crowd.

3 Café del Born Nou
Pl Comercial 10

Located opposite the El born Centre de Cultura i Memòriaon, this café offers good coffee and cakes, and a decent range of salads, sandwiches and light meals. It attracts a relaxed, arty crowd who linger over their newspapers and fast WiFi.

4 Milk
MAP M5 ■ C/Gignàs 21

Decorated like a luxurious living room with elegant sofas, golden picture frames, chandeliers and 1950s-style wallpaper, Milk serves brunch (from 9am to 4:30pm), lunch and dinner daily.

5 Ginger
MAP N4 ■ C/Palma de Sant Just 1 ■ Closed Sun & Mon

An elegant bar that serves fine wines, champagne, *cava*, cocktails and a variety of creative tapas to a glamorous crowd.

6 Glaciar
MAP L4 ■ Pl Reial 3

Occupying a prime corner of Plaça Reial, this atmospheric café-bar brings in all types. Grab a spot on the terrace for a front-row view of activities on the *plaça*.

7 La Vinya del Senyor
MAP N5 ■ Pl Santa Maria 5

A classy yet cosy bar, attracting wine lovers from all over the city who come to sample a rich array of Spanish and international varieties.

8 Collage Art & Cocktail Social Club
MAP N5 ■ C/Consellers 4

Creative experimentation, including molecular "cocktelery", at this unique bar produces highly original cocktails at good prices. The lounge upstairs has vintage furniture and an old piano, and hosts pocket-size painting exhibitions.

9 Juanra Falces
MAP P4 ■ C/Rec 24 ■ Closed Sun & Mon

The original cocktail bar in El Born, the intimate, 1950s-style Juanra Falces pours excellent (read: potent) cocktails for locals.

10 Mudanzas
MAP P5 ■ C/Vidrieria 15

This long-time favourite has circular marble tables, black-and-white tiled floors and an informal "everybody's welcome" vibe.

The living-room decor at Milk

Clubs and Music Venues

 Jamboree
MAP L4 ■ Pl Reial 17 ■ Adm
■ www.masimas.com/jamboree
This Barri Gòtic institution has live jazz every night (8pm–midnight). It then morphs into a dance club, with DJs spinning everything from hip-hop to R&B and salsa *(see p58)*.

 Tarantos
MAP L4 ■ Pl Reial 17 ■ Adm
■ www.masimas.com
Next door to Jamboree, Tarantos is the oldest flamenco club in Barcelona. It has three daily perform-ances of flamenco guitar playing, singing and dancing – at 8:30, 9:30 and 10:30pm – by local emerging artists and occasional big names.

3 Sidecar Factory Club
MAP L4 ■ Pl Reial 7 ■ Adm
■ Closed Sun
Barcelona's music scene is like a motorcycle to which Sidecar is inseparably bound. Partygoers come for music, cabaret and good food.

Performance at the Harlem Jazz Club

4 Harlem Jazz Club
MAP M5 ■ C/Comtessa de Sobradiel 8 ■ Closed Mon, concerts from 10:30pm ■ Adm
■ www.harlemjazzclub.es
Dark and smoky, this kick-back jazz haunt showcases a choice line-up of jazz and blues, flamenco fusion, reggae and African music *(see p54)*.

5 Sor Rita Bar
MAP L5 ■ C/Mercè 27
A fun bar that features fantastically kitsch and colourful decor.

The 1980s-style Polaroids bar

6 Polaroids
MAP M5 ■ C/Còdols 29
A fabulously quirky bar with 80s-style decor and great retro sounds. Drinks are well priced and usually come with big bowls of free popcorn. Be sure to get here early – the place is always packed.

7 El Paraigua
MAP E4 ■ C/l Pas de l'Ensenyança 2 ■ Adm ■ www.elparaigua.com
This pretty *fin de siècle* café has an intimate basement venue that stages live music from jazz to folk and blues.

8 Café Royale
MAP L5 ■ C/Nou de Zurbano 3
■ Closed Sun & Mon
With a great location next to the Plaça Reial, this club has minimalist, elegant decor and a small dance floor. There are occasional live music and flamenco concerts.

9 Marula Café
MAP L5 ■ C/Escudellers 49
An intimate club featuring local and international DJs and upbeat live music every day of the week.

10 Karma
MAP L4 ■ Pl Reial 10 ■ Adm
■ Closed Mon
The hippie origins and 1970s glamour of this club are as popular with partygoers as ever.

See map on pp76–7

Cafés and Light Eats

(1) Cafè d'Estiu
MAP N3 ▪ Pl de Sant Iu 5–6
▪ 93 310 30 14 ▪ Closed Mon

This terrace café on the patio of the Museu Frederic Marès *(see p78)* is replete with stone pillars, climbing ivy and orange trees. Your museum ticket entitles you to a discount.

(2) La Báscula
MAP P4 ▪ C/Flassaders 30
▪ 93 319 98 66 ▪ Closed Mon & Tue

This quirky café in an old chocolate factory has several vegetarian dishes and a range of tasty cakes.

(3) Cafè-Bar L'Antiquari
MAP N4 ▪ C/Veguer 13
▪ 93 461 95 89

By day, sit by the window and enjoy views of the medieval old town. By night, sip cocktails in the Baroque-inspired upstairs lounge.

(4) Elsa y Freda
MAP F4 & Q2 ▪ C/Rec Comtal 11 ▪ 93 501 66 11

With its leather armchairs and big windows, this is the perfect place to enjoy a long, lazy brunch, with dishes ranging from classic *patates braves* to salmon sushi.

(5) Tetería Salterio
MAP M4 ▪ C/Sant Domenec del Call 4 ▪ 93 302 50 28 ▪ Closed until 1pm Sat & Sun

Enjoy tea and sweet Arab cakes. Don't miss the *sardo*, an Oriental-style pizza with a variety of fillings.

(6) Café Bliss
MAP N4 ▪ Pl Sant Just ▪ 93 268 10 22

Stop at this delightful café for a break while exploring the Barri Gòtic. It offers divine cakes, light meals, snacks and coffee. Ask for an outside table in summer *(see p64)*.

(7) En Apartè
MAP P2 ▪ C/Lluís el Piadós 2
▪ 93 269 13 35

A relaxing option with outside tables overlooking the square serving French dishes and wines, good coffee and brunch *(see p65)*.

(8) Caelum
MAP M3 ▪ C/Palla 8
▪ 93 302 69 93

Upstairs sells honey, preserves and other foods made in convents and monasteries all over Spain. Downstairs you can sample the delicacies on the site of 15th-century baths.

(9) La Granja Pallaresa
MAP L3 ▪ C/Petritxol 11
▪ 93 302 20 36 ▪ Closed from 1–4pm daily, 1–5pm Sun

This family-run *xocolateria* has long been serving up thick, dark hot chocolate with *xurros* (fried, sugary dough strips) for dunking.

(10) Bar del Pla
MAP P4 ▪ C/Montcada 2
▪ 93 268 30 03 ▪ Closed Sun

Savour Spanish tapas with a French twist. Try the pig's trotters with *foie gras* or the squid ink croquettes.

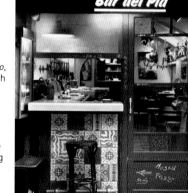

Entrance to Bar del Pla

Restaurants and Tapas Bars

 Bar Mundial
MAP P3 ■ Pl de Sant Agustí
Vell 1 ■ 93 319 90 56 ■ Closed Mon
and lunch Tue ■ €

Opened in 1925 and still boasting the original marble tables, this classic tapas bar is one of the best. The menu changes constantly.

2 Cal Pep
MAP P5 ■ Pl de les Olles 8
■ 93 310 79 61 ■ Closed Sun, Mon
lunch, Aug ■ €€

Taste a variety of delicious tapas, including the finest seafood, at this busy, established eatery.

3 Cafè de l'Acadèmia
MAP N4 ■ C/Lledó 1 ■ 93 319
82 53 ■ Closed Sat, Sun, Aug ■ €€

Located in an 18th-century building, this excellent restaurant serves superb modern Catalan cuisine and top-notch desserts.

4 Casa Delfín
MAP F5 ■ Passeig del Born 36
■ 93 319 30 88 ■ Open until midnight
daily (1am Fri, Sat) ■ €€

This pretty bistro uses seasonal produce in imaginative dishes and tapas. The fried artichokes with *romesco* sauce are a must.

5 Llamber
MAP F4 & P4 ■ C/Fusina 5
■ 93 319 62 50 ■ €€

Enjoy fresh seasonal produce – including vegetables from their own garden and Mediterranean red prawns – in a cool, loft-style interior with exposed brickwork and warm woodwork adding to the atmosphere.

 Agut
MAP M5 ■ C/Gignàs 16
■ 93 315 17 09 ■ Closed Sun dinner &
Mon, 1 week in Jan, Aug ■ €€

Established in 1924, this friendly family restaurant has been delighting patrons with excellent Catalan cuisine at reasonable prices.

PRICE CATEGORIES

For a three-course meal for one with half a bottle of wine (or equivalent meal), including taxes and extra charges.

....

€ under €35   €€ €35–50   €€€ over €50

7 Bodega La Palma
MAP M4 ■ Palma de Sant Just 7
■ 93 315 06 56 ■ Closed Sun ■ €

This bohemian restaurant in a former wine cellar offers a delicious choice of tapas, including stuffed Piquillo peppers.

The elegant interior of Raso Terra

8 Raso Terra
MAP M4 ■ C/Palau 5
■ 93 318 69 26 ■ Closed Mon ■ €€

Proponents of the slow food movement, the owners of this stylish, loft-style restaurant serve delicious vegetarian and vegan dishes along with organic wines and beer.

9 El Xampanyet
MAP P4 ■ C/Montcada 22
■ 93 319 70 03 ■ Closed Sun
evening & Mon ■ €

An old-fashioned bar popular for its *cava* and range of simple tapas.

10 Govinda
MAP M2 ■ Pl Vila de Madrid 4
■ 93 318 77 29 ■ Closed Sun & Mon
evenings ■ €

This laid-back eatery serves up vegetarian Indian main dishes and delectable desserts, but no alcohol.

See map on pp76–7

🔟 El Raval

The sleek Museu d'Art Contemporani (MACBA) sits near ramshackle tenements; Asian groceries sell spices next to what were once Europe's most decadent brothels; art galleries share narrow streets with smoky old bars – this is a traditional working-class neighbourhood in flux. Since the 1990s it has been undergoing an enthusiastic urban renewal. Not surprisingly, this has sparked a real-estate boom that is now acting as a magnet for the city's young, hip crowd.

Chimney, Palau Güell

EL RAVAL

0 metres 200
0 yards 200

1 Top 10 Sights
see pp86–9

1 Good-Value Eats
see p93

1 Vintage and Second-Hand Shops see p91

1 Bars and Clubs
see p92

1 Galleries and Design Shops see p90

1 Museu d'Art Contemporani (MACBA)

This dramatic, glass-fronted building was designed by American architect Richard Meier. An eclectic array of work by a host of big-name Spanish and international artists is gathered in this contemporary art mecca *(see pp34–5)*. Excellent temporary exhibitions display everything from mixed media to sculpture and photography. Opposite stands the Gothic-style 16th-century Convent dels Àngels, originally built by Bartomeu Roig for the Dominican Tertiary Sisters. This is now used by Capella MACBA for temporary exhibitions, but long-term plans are to extend the galleries and exhibit some of MACBA's collection here permanently.

2 Centre de Cultura Contemporània (CCCB)

Housed in the 18th-century Casa de la Caritat, the CCCB is a focal point for the city's thriving contemporary art scene *(see pp34–5)*. It hosts innovative art exhibitions, literature festivals, film screenings and lectures. A medieval courtyard is dazzlingly offset by a massive angled glass wall, artfully designed to reflect the city's skyline.

The stark white exterior of MACBA

3 Museu Marítim

MAP K6 ■ Av de les Drassanes ■ 10am–8pm daily ■ Adm, free from 3pm every Sun ■ Santa Eulàlia sailing trips: 10am–1pm Sat (advance reservations needed) ■ www.mmb.cat

Barcelona's seafaring legacy comes to life at this museum *(see p43)*, which reopened in 2015 with new high-tech displays after renovations. Admire the dramatic Gothic arches, where the royal ships were once built, and the full-scale replica of the *Real*, a 16th-century fighting galley. You can also explore the *Santa Eulàlia (see p102)*, a 1918 schooner moored at the Moll de la Fusta, and even take a sailing trip in her around the seafront on Saturdays.

4 Palau Güell

MAP L4 ■ C/Nou de la Rambla 3–5 ■ Open 10am–8pm Tue–Sun (to 5:30pm Nov–Mar); last entry 1 hr before closing ■ Adm ■ www.palauguell.cat

In 1886, Count Güell asked Gaudí to build him a mansion that would set him apart from his neighbours. The result is the Palau Güell, one of Gaudí's earliest commissions. The interior is darker and less playful than his later works, but stained-glass panels and windows make the most of the light. The rooms are arranged around a huge central salon topped with a domed ceiling. The charming roof terrace hints at the glorious rooftops like La Pedrera.

Sumptuous interior of Palau Güell

5 Carrers dels Tallers and de la Riera Baixa
MAP L1 & K3

Looking for vintage blue-and-white French navy tops once favoured by the likes of Picasso or bootleg CDs of Madonna's European tour? Along Carrers dels Tallers and de la Riera Baixa in the heart of El Raval are several vintage music and clothing shops selling everything from vinyl and the latest CDs to original Hawaiian shirts. On Saturdays, Carrer de la Riera Baixa has its own market (11am–9pm), when its stores display their wares on the street.

6 Avinguda Paral·lel
MAP B3–D5

This long avenue was home to the city's liveliest theatre and cabaret halls at the turn of the 20th century, and, despite being badly bombed in the Civil War, it remains the centre of the theatre district. The area is currently undergoing a resurgence, spearheaded by the restoration of the landmark El Molino music hall, which dates from 1898 and is once again a venue for concerts and shows (see p54). The street hosts a number of festivals and there are plans to turn the century-old Teatro Arnau into a museum of the performing arts.

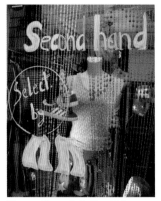

Shop on Carrer de la Riera Baixa

7 La Rambla del Raval
MAP K4

This pedestrian walkway, lined with palm trees, started as an attempt by city planners to spark a similar environment to that of the famed La Rambla (see pp16–17). The striking, conical Barceló Hotel, and its panoramic rooftop terrace, and the sleek Filmoteca, a film archive complete with café and cinema, are signs of the area's gentrification. Halfway down the street, Botero's huge, plump bronze *Cat* usually has several neighbourhood kids crawling over its back. Trendy bars and cafés mean the Rambla del Raval rivals its more famous cousin for snacking and people-watching.

8 Filmoteca
MAP K4 ▪ Pl de Salvador Seguí 1–9 ▪ 93 567 10 70 ▪ www. filmoteca.cat

The Filmoteca – the Catalan film archive – occupies a huge, sleek contemporary building just off the Rambla del Raval and has played a large part in the ongoing regeneration of this neighbourhood. It has two screening rooms and shows a varied and interesting programme. This includes film cycles dedicated to the finest directors from around the world, documentaries, plenty of Catalonia works, and special events for children. It's extremely popular,

Buildings on Avinguda Paral·lel

not least because prices are very reasonable. There is also a great café which has a library, a documentation centre and an in-demand outdoor terrace. On the first Sunday of the month, a flea market is held in the square outside.

⑨ Antic Hospital de la Santa Creu

MAP K3 ■ Entrances on C/Carme and at C/Hospital 56 ■ Courtyard open 9am–8pm daily

This Gothic hospital complex, now home to the National Library and various cultural organizations, dates from 1401 and is a reminder of the neighbourhood's medieval past. Visitors can wander in a pleasant garden surrounded by Gothic pillars, but a reader's card is needed for admission to the library. The chapel has been converted into a wonderful contemporary art space (see p90).

⑩ Església de Sant Pau del Camp

MAP J4 ■ C/Sant Pau 101 ■ Open 10am–1:30pm & 4–7:30pm Mon–Fri, 9:30am–12:30pm Sat; Mass 8pm Sat, noon Sun ■ Adm

Deep in the heart of El Raval is this Romanesque church, one of the oldest in Barcelona. Originally founded as a Benedictine monastery in the 9th century and subsequently rebuilt, this ancient church boasts 12th-century cloister (see p40).

Església de Sant Pau del Camp

A RAMBLE IN EL RAVAL

▶ MORNING

Choose an exhibition that appeals at either **MACBA** or the **CCCB** (see p87), the city's two most important institutions of contemporary art and culture, which sit right next to each other. Watch the skateboarders on the Plaça dels Àngels or relax in the café overlooking the courtyard. Take C/Joaquin Costa down to the **Rambla del Raval** where you can stroll beneath the palm trees and admire Fernando Botero's *Cat*. The Rambla is crammed with cafés and restaurants: pick one for lunch, or head to the popular café in the **Filmoteca**, located just off the Rambla.

AFTERNOON

At the bottom of the Rambla, turn right on C/Sant Pau towards the charming Romanesque monastery of **Església Sant Pau del Camp**. Admire the simple church and its miniature cloister with delicately-carved columns. Then walk back along C/Sant Pau, turning right when you reach the Rambla, then left on C/Nou de la Rambla. At no. 3 stands Gaudí's remarkable **Palau Güell**, an extravagant mansion that was one of his first commissions for the Güells. It has been beautifully restored, with its lavish salons and charming rooftop open to visitors. Kick off the evening with an absinthe at one of Barcelona's oldest bars, the **Marsella** (p92), before heading to the nearby **London Bar** (p92), which boasts original *Modernista* decor.

See map on p86 ←

Galleries and Design Shops

1 Galeria dels Àngels
MAP L2 ■ C/Pintor Fortuny 27
■ Closed Sat & Sun

Emerging and established artists –
local and foreign – are shown at this
cutting-edge contemporary painting,
photography and sculpture gallery.

2 Miscelanea
MAP K5 ■ C/Guardia 10
■ Open 5–11pm Wed–Sun (to
midnight Fri & Sat), closed Aug
■ www.miscelanea.info

Miscelanea is an artists' project
with a multidisciplinary space.
At the entrance is a gallery, hosting
temporary exhibitions by emerging
local and international
artists. Downstairs is a
shop, selling design
objects, original arts
and prints, and
above the shop is a
café with free Wi-Fi.

Fish, Imanol Ossa

3 Siesta
MAP K2 ■ C/Ferlandina 18 ■ 93
317 80 41 ■ Closed Sat pm, Sun & Mon

Part boutique, part art gallery,
this shop sells unique ceramics,
jewellery and glass art. It also
hosts temporary exhibitions.

4 Tinta Invisible
MAP K1 ■ C/Lleó 6 ■ 93 301
29 42 ■ Closed Sat–Sun

This workshop and gallery is
dedicated to "artists of the book".
On show are engravings, book-
binding, prints and graphic design.

Illustrations at Tinta Invisible

5 Grey Street
MAP D4 ■ C/Peu de la Creu 25
■ Open noon–9pm Mon–Sat

This lovingly-curated shop, run by an
expat Australian, sells a selection of
mostly locally-made gifts and crafts,
from stationery to jewellery and bags.

6 La Capella
MAP K3 ■ C/Hospital 56
■ Opening times vary, check website
■ www.lacapella.bcn.cat

This Gothic chapel at the Antic
Hospital de la Santa Creu (see p89)
is now a contemporary art gallery
run by the city and dedicated to
emerging artists (see p70).

7 Imanol Ossa
MAP D4 & K2
■ C/Peu de la Creu 24
■ 63 68 05 703
■ www.imanolossa.com

Original lamps, jewellery,
and mobiles are made
from all kinds of upcycled treasures
at this studio, run by a young designer.

8 La Xina A.R.T.
MAP J4 ■ C/Hort de la Bomba 6
■ Open 5:30–8:30pm Thu–Sat
■ www.laxinaart.org

The latest contemporary art features
at this innovative gallery started by
four local artists in the late 1990s.

9 NuOvum
MAP L2 ■ C/Pintor Fortuny 30
■ Closed Sun

Some unusual designs – from
jewellery to paintings to lamps – are
all on display in this eclectic shop.

10 Room Service
MAP E4 ■ C/dels Àngels 16
■ 93 302 10 16 ■ Open 11am–2pm
& 4:30–7pm Mon–Fri; closed Aug
■ www.roomsd.com

This commercial gallery is dedicated
to cutting-edge design, principally
for the home. International creators
are represented, along with up-and-
coming local talent.

Vintage and Second-Hand Shops

1 **Flamingos**
MAP D4 & K2 ■ C/de
Ferlandina 20 ■ 93 182 43 87
■ Open 11am–9pm Mon–Sat
■ www.vintagekilo.com

This fabulous vintage store, also selling old posters and bric-a-brac, operates on a weight system: you pay per kilo, depending on the clothing category you choose.

2 **Holala**
MAP L1 ■ C/Tallers 73
■ Open 11am–9pm Mon–Sat

Rummage for an outfit at this three-floor vintage store, with everything from original silk kimonos to army pants and colourful 1950s bathing suits.

3 **Fusta'm**
MAP K1 ■ C/Joaquim Costa
62 ■ Open 11am–2pm & 5–8:30pm
Mon–Sat ■ www.fustam.cat

Discover second-hand furniture, lighting and decorative objects from around the world in 1950s, 60s and 70s styles, all of them completely restored at their own workshop.

4 **Revólver Records**
MAP L2 ■ C/Tallers 11
■ Closed Sun

The speciality here is classic rock – the wall art depicts The Rolling Stones and Jimi Hendrix. One floor houses CDs, the other vinyl.

5 **Wilde Vintage**
MAP K2 ■ C/Joaquin Costa 2

This dimly-lit boudoiresque boutique is lined with vintage sunglasses, from aviator shades to pairs of cat's-eye specs from the 1960s.

6 **Holala Plaza**
MAP L1 ■ Pl Castella 2
■ Closed Sun

This huge shop in the heart of the Raval sells second-hand clothes, furniture and bric-a-brac.

A vintage furniture store in Barri Gotic

7 **La Principal**
MAP K1 ■ C/Valldonzella 52
■ 60 726 57 57 ■ www.laprincipal
retro.com

Set in a charming old dairy, this chic boutique has a fantastic range of vintage clothing for men and women.

8 **Soul BCN**
MAP L1 ■ C/Tallers 15
■ 93 481 32 94

A vintage-style shop selling 1950s frocks, cats'-eye sunglasses, flirty Bardot tops and much more.

9 **Discos Tesla**
MAP L2 ■ C/Tallers 3

This small but well-stocked record and CD store focuses on alternative music from decades past. Visitors can hum a few lines of a song and the owner will track it down.

10 **The Vintage Room**
MAP D4 ■ C/Peu de la Creu
16 bis ■ 647 63 26 94 ■ Open noon–2:30pm & 5–8pm Tue–Sat, closed
Sat in Aug

Furniture and home decor from the 1950s to 1970s is sold in this funky showroom. Smaller pieces include light fittings, lamps and ceramics mostly from Italy and Germany.

See map on p86 ←

Bars and Clubs

Bar Almirall, founded in 1860

1 Bar Almirall
MAP K2 ■ C/Joaquin Costa 33

The *Modernista* doors swing open to a young, friendly crowd at the city's oldest watering hole. Founded in 1860, the bar has many original fittings, plus eclectic music and strong cocktails.

2 Zelig
MAP K2 ■ C/Carme 116

Intimate and welcoming, this gay-friendly bar is a great place to start the night. There are excellent cocktails – including a great mojito – and light snacks.

3 Bar Resolis
MAP K3 ■ C/Riera Baixa 22

Formerly an old-fashioned neighbourhood bar, this is now an appealing boho-chic tavern with a small terrace. Wine and cocktails accompany delicious tapas.

4 Marsella
MAP K4 ■ C/Sant Pau 65

This dimly lit *Modernista* bar serves up cocktails and absinthe to regulars and first-timers *(see p58)*.

5 Ultramarinos
MAP E5 ■ Las Ramblas 31

Once a cinema, this huge space has been converted into a drinking and dining destination with bright graphics and retro furniture. It serves creative share plates – try the tuna *tataki* – and an excellent selection of cocktails.

6 Betty Ford's
MAP K1 ■ C/Joaquin Costa 56

Named after the Hollywood set's favourite rehab and detox centre, this kitsch, laid-back cocktail bar has a soothing 1950s chill-out vibe.

7 Moog
MAP L5 ■ C/Arc del Teatre 3

Big-name DJs spin techno and electronica, but for a boogie to classic 1980s hits, head for the second floor.

8 Boadas Cocktail Bar
MAP L2 ■ C/Tallers 1
■ Closed Sun

This smooth little cocktail bar, founded in 1933, continues to mix the meanest martinis in town for an elbow-to-elbow crowd.

9 Jazz Sí Club
MAP D4 ■ C/ Requesens 2

This bar-club puts on live gigs, from jazz (Wednesdays), to Cuban (Thursdays), flamenco (Fridays and Saturdays) and pop-rock (Tuesdays and Sundays). There is a €10 cover charge, which includes a drink.

10 London Bar
MAP K4 ■ C/Nou de la Rambla 34 ■ Closed Mon

This cluttered bar has long been *de rigueur*, once with the likes of Picasso, Hemingway and Miró. Sip cocktails and enjoy the original *Modernista* furnishings.

Modernista decor at the London Bar

Good-Value Eats

1 Caravelle
MAP E4 ▪ C/Pintor Fortuny 31
▪ 93 317 98 92 ▪ Closed Mon eve ▪ €

This spot near the MACBA museum has become a favourite for weekend brunch and long coffee breaks. The menu changes regularly but is likely to include delicious huevos rancheros, filling soups and creative salads. Lots of vegetarian options too.

2 Can Lluís
MAP J3 ▪ C/de la Cera 49
▪ 93 441 11 87 ▪ Closed Sun ▪ €€

This restaurant, run by three consecutive generations, has been preparing its family recipes since 1929. The food is simple but delicious, and the fixed-price lunch menu is a bargain.

3 Ca l'Isidre
MAP J4 ▪ C/Les Flors 12 ▪ 93 441 11 39 ▪ Closed Sat (in summer), Sun, Easter, 2 weeks in Aug, Christmas ▪ €€€

Picasso, Tapiès, Miró, Dalí, Woody Allen and even King Juan Carlos have dined on the delicious Catalan fare at this popular artists' hang-out.

4 Teresa Carles
MAP L1 ▪ C/Jovellanos 2
▪ 93 317 18 29 ▪ €

Come here for excellent, imaginative vegetarian fare, such as crêpes with artichokes and brie. The set lunch Monday–Friday is great value.

5 El Colectivo Café
MAP L2 ▪ C/Pintor Fortuny 22
▪ 93 318 63 80 ▪ Closed Sun in Aug ▪ €

A quiet, modern café serving good coffee and some of the best cakes in town, including vegan options.

6 Tàber Café
MAP K2 ▪ C/Joaquin Costa 47 ▪ 63 451 65 47 ▪ Open from noon Mon–Sat, from 5pm Sun ▪ €

This small, but welcoming café serves great coffee, along with smoothies, juices and homemade cakes.

PRICE CATEGORIES

For a three-course meal for one with half a bottle of wine (or equivalent meal), including taxes and extra charges.

€ under €35   €€ €35–50   €€€ over €50

7 Bacaro
MAP L3 ▪ C/Jerusalén 6
▪ Closed Sun ▪ 69 579 60 66 ▪ €€

Tucked behind the Boqueria market, this convivial little Italian restaurant-bar serves a frequently-changing menu of modern Venetian cuisine.

The bar at Marmalade

8 Marmalade
MAP J2 ▪ C/Riera Alta 4–6
▪ 93 442 39 66 ▪ €

A loft-style bar providing cocktails, snacks and meals in the evenings (stir fries, fajitas, fish and chips), plus a great brunch at weekends.

9 Els Ocellets
MAP D4 ▪ Ronda Sant Pau 55
▪ 93 441 10 46 ▪ Closed Sun eve, Mon, 2 weeks in Aug ▪ €

Traditional cuisine with a creative touch in elegant surroundings. Good value fixed-price menus.

10 L'Havana
MAP K2 ▪ C/Lleó 1 ▪ 93 302 21 06 ▪ Closed Sun eve, Mon, 2 weeks in Aug ▪ €€

Despite the name, this eatery serves superb Catalan cuisine. Try the fresh fish of the day or classic Catalan dishes such as pig's trotters.

See map on p86 ←

🔟 Montjuïc

Named the "Jewish Mountain" after an important Jewish cemetery that existed here in the Middle Ages, this sizable park was first landscaped for the 1929 International Exhibition, when the Palau Nacional and the Mies van der Rohe Pavilion were also built. However, the area soon fell into general disuse, becoming synonymous with decline. With the grim shadow left by the castle, which for years acted as a slaughterhouse for Franco's firing squads, it is little short of miraculous that Montjuïc is now one of the city's biggest draws. As the site for the 1992 Olympics, it was transformed into a beautiful green oasis, with fabulous museums and sports facilities all connected by a network of outdoor escalators and interlaced with quiet, shady gardens.

Statue, Castell de Montjuïc

1 Palau Nacional and Museu Nacional d'Art de Catalunya

The Palau Nacional is home to the Museu Nacional d'Art de Catalunya, which exhibits Catalonia's historic art collections. Boasting one of Europe's finest displays of Romanesque art, the museum includes a series of 12th-century frescoes, rescued from Catalan Pyrenean churches and painstakingly reassembled in a series of galleries (see pp20–1).

2 Fundació Joan Miró

One of Catalonia's most acclaimed painters and sculptors, Joan Miró (1893–1983) donated many of the 11,000 works held by the museum. Housed in a stark white building designed by his friend, architect Josep Lluís Sert, this is the world's most complete collection of Miró's work (see pp28–9).

3 Font Màgica

MAP B4 ▪ Pl Carles Buigas 1 (off Av Reina Maria Cristina) ▪ Apr, May & Oct: 9pm & 9:30pm Thu–Sat; Jun–Sep: 9:30pm & 10pm Wed–Sun; Nov–Mar: 8pm & 8:30pm Thu–Sat; no shows Jan & Feb

Below the cascades and fountains that decend from the Palau Nacional is the Magic Fountain, designed by Carles Buigas for the International Exhibition of 1929. As darkness descends, countless jets of water are choreographed in a mesmerizing sound and light show. When the water meets in a single jet it can soar to

Font Màgica's soaring jets of water

15 m (50 ft). The extravagant finale is often accompanied by a recording of Freddie Mercury and soprano Montserrat Caballé singing the anthem *Barcelona* as the water fades from pink to green and back to white (see p70). The Four Columns behind the fountain represent the Catalan flag and are a symbol of the Catalanism movement.

4 Castell de Montjuïc

MAP B6 ▪ Carretera de Montjuïc 66 ▪ Open 10am–6pm daily (to 8pm Apr–Oct) ▪ Adm ▪ ajuntament. barcelona.cat/castelldemontjuic/en

Dominating Montjuïc's hill, this gloomy castle was once a prison and torture centre for political prisoners. At the end of the Spanish Civil War, 4,000 Catalan nationalists and republicans were shot in the nearby Fossar de la Pedrera. After such a tragic history, the castle is entering a happier phase: it has been developed into an international peace centre. Visitors can still climb the fort's sturdy bastions for superb views of the port below.

Castell de Montjuïc

The atmospheric Teatre Grec

5 Teatre Grec
MAP C4 ■ Pg Santa Madrona
■ Open for visits 10am–dusk daily
■ Free when there are no shows
■ www.lameva.barcelona.cat/grec/
el-teatre-grec

This beautiful amphitheatre (see p54) was inspired by the Classical ideas of what was known as *Noucentisme*. This late 19th-century Catalan architectural movement was a reaction to the overly-decorative nature of *Modernisme*. With its leafy green backdrop and beautiful gardens, there are few places more enchanting than this to watch *Swan Lake* or listen to some jazz. The open-air theatre is used for shows during the summertime Grec Festival (see p73), when it also becomes home to a luxurious outdoor restaurant.

6 Estadi Olímpic
MAP B5 ■ Av de l'Estadi 60
■ Museum: open 10am–6pm (to 8pm Apr–Sep) Tue–Sat, 10am–2:30pm Sun; stadium can be viewed from upper levels ■ Adm for museum

The stadium was first built for the 1936 Workers' Olympics, which were cancelled with the outbreak of the Spanish Civil War (see pp38–9).

The original Neo-Classical façade is still in place, but the stadium was rebuilt for the 1992 Olympic Games (see p39). The interactive Museu Olímpic i de l'Esport nearby is dedicated to all aspects of sport.

7 Pavelló Mies van der Rohe
MAP B4 ■ Av Francesc Ferrer i Guàrdia 7 ■ Open 10am–8pm daily ■ Adm (free for under-16s)

You might wonder exactly what this box-like pavilion of stone, marble, onyx and glass is doing in the middle of Montjuïc's monumental architecture. Years ahead of its time, this architectural gem was Germany's contribution to the 1929 International Exhibition. Built by Ludwig Mies van der Rohe (1886–1969), the Rationalist pavilion was soon demolished, only to be reconstructed in 1986. Inside, the elegant sculpture *Morning* by Georg Kolbe (1877–1947) is reflected in a small lake.

8 Palau Sant Jordi
MAP A4 ■ Pg Olímpic 5–7
■ Open 10am–6pm (to 8pm May–Sep) Sat & Sun

The biggest star of all the Olympic facilities is this steel-and-glass indoor stadium and multipurpose installation designed by Japanese architect Arata Isozaki. Holding around 17,000 people, the stadium is the home of the city's basketball team. The esplanade – a surreal forest of concrete and metal pillars – was designed by Aiko Isozaki, Arata's wife. Further down the hill are the indoor and outdoor Bernat Picornell Olympic pools, both of which are open to the public.

Palau Sant Jordi

9 Poble Espanyol

MAP A3 ■ Av Francesc Ferrer
i Guàrdia ■ Open 9am–8pm Mon,
9am–midnight Tue–Thu & Sun,
9am–3am Fri, 9am–4pm Sat ■ Adm

This Spanish *poble* (village) features
a hotchpotch of famous buildings and
streets from around Spain recreated
in full-scale. Although a bit tacky, it
has become a centre for arts and
crafts, including an impressive glass-
blowers' workshop, and is one of the
city's most popular attractions. There
are restaurants and cafés aplenty, as
well as a couple of trendy nightclubs
(see p59).

Traditional alleys of Poble Espanyol

10 CaixaForum

MAP B3 ■ Av Francesc Ferrer
i Guàrdia 6–8 ■ Open 10am–8pm
daily (to 11pm on Wed in Jul & Aug)
■ Adm

The Fundació La Caixa's impressive
collection of contemporary art is
housed in a former textile factory
built in 1911 by Catalan *Modernista*
architect Puig i Cadafalch. Restored
and opened as a gallery in 2002,
it assembles some 800 works by
Spanish and foreign artists, shown
in rotation along with temporary
international exhibitions.

A DAY IN MONTJUÏC

▶ **MORNING**

To get to the **Fundació Joan Miró**
(see pp28–9) before the crowds
and with energy to spare, hop
on the funicular from Parallel
metro station. It is a short
walk from the funicular to the
museum, where you'll need
an hour and a half to absorb
the impressive collection of
Miró paintings, sketches and
sculptures. When you've had
your fill of contemporary art,
refuel with a *cafè amb llet (see
p65)* on the restaurant terrace
before backtracking along Av
de Miramar and jumping on
the cable car up to **Castell de
Montjuïc** *(see p95)*. Wander the
castle gardens and look out over
the city and the bustling docks.
Return to Av de Miramar by cable
car and follow the signs to
Palau Nacional *(see p95)*, where
you can lunch on typical Catalan
cuisine with a modern twist at
the elegant Òleum *(see p99)*.

AFTERNOON

After lunch, spend time admiring
the extraordinary Romanesque
art collection at MNAC *(see
pp22–3)*. When you exit, turn
right and follow the signs to
the Olympic complex. The **Estadi
Olímpic** is worth a look, but the
silver-domed **Palau Sant Jordi**
steals the limelight. Spend the
late afternoon cooling down with
a dip in the fantastic open-air
pool at nearby **Bernat Picornell**.
From here it is a short stroll to
the **Poble Espanyol**, where you
can settle in at a terrace bar in
Plaça Major.

See map on p94 ←

Parks and Gardens

1 Jardins Mossèn Costa i Llobera
MAP C5

These are among Europe's most important cactus and succulent gardens. They are particularly impressive as the sun sets, when surreal shapes and shadows emerge.

2 Jardí Botànic
MAP A5 ■ Open Oct–Mar: 10am–5pm daily; Apr–Sep: 10am–7pm daily ■ Adm (free first Sun of month, every Sun after 3pm) ■ www.museuciencies.cat

Barcelona's botanical gardens are found among the stadiums used in the Olympics of 1992. Dating from 1999, they boast hundreds of examples of typical Mediterranean flora. Don't miss the charming Jardí Botànic Històric nearby *(see p71)*.

3 Jardins Mossèn Cinto Verdaguer
MAP C5

The best time to visit these wonderfully elegant gardens is during spring, when the plants are in blossom and the colours and scents are in full force.

4 Jardins del Castell
MAP B5

Cannons dotted among the rose bushes and pathways along the walls of a flower-filled moat are the highlights of these gardens which ring the castle.

5 Jardins del Teatre Grec
MAP C4

Reminiscent of the Hanging Gardens of Babylon, this gracious oasis surrounding the Greek amphitheatre is officially known as La Rosadela.

6 Jardins de Miramar
MAP C5

Opposite the Miramar, these gardens are scattered with stairways leading to enchanting leafy groves with vistas across the city and the port area.

7 Jardins Laribal
MAP B4

This multilevel park hides a small *Modernista* house by architect Puig i Cadafalch and the Font del Gat, a drinking fountain which has inspired many local songs.

8 Jardins de Joan Maragall
MAP B4 ■ Open 10am–3pm Sat & Sun

An avenue lined with sculptures by Frederic Marès and Ernest Maragall is the main delight in the Jardins de Joan Maragall, which also has the last of the city's *ginjoler* trees.

Statue, Jardins de Joan Maragall

9 Jardins de Joan Brossa
MAP C5

These beautiful gardens come into their own in spring, but are popular year-round with kids thanks to the musical instruments, climbing frames and a flying fox.

10 El Mirador del Llobregat
MAP A3

A viewing area with small gardens nearby, this is the only place in the city where you can see the plains of the Llobregat stretching below.

Restaurants, Cafés and Bars

1 Òleum
MAP B4 ▪ Palau Nacional
▪ 93 289 06 79 ▪ Closed Sun, Tue,
Wed & Thu eves & Mon ▪ €€

Dine on refined Mediterranean
cuisine at this elegant venue under
the dome of the Palau Nacional –
home of the Museu Nacional d'Art
de Catalunya – and enjoy the views
across the city.

2 Bar Seco
MAP C5 ▪ Pg Montjuïc 74
▪ 93 329 63 74 ▪ Closed Sun eve ▪ €

A simple café serving cakes, snacks
and more substantial dishes at
lunchtime. There's a summer
terrace and free Wi-Fi.

3 El Sortidor
MAP C4 ▪ Pl del Sortidor 5
▪ 63 634 26 11 ▪ Closed Mon eve,
Tue eve ▪ €

Boasting original stained-glass
doors and tiled floors from 1908,
El Sortidor serves elegant meals
to match the romantic setting.

4 La Tomaquera
MAP C4 ▪ C/Margarit 58
▪ Closed Sun dinner, Mon, Aug,
Easter week ▪ €

A classic neighbourhood restaurant
that offers up delicious Catalan home
cooking at bargain prices. The snails
served here are considered the best
in town.

5 El Lliure
MAP B4 ▪ Pg Santa Madrona
40-46 ▪ Open lunch Mon–Fri, dinner
on days with performances ▪ €

The Lliure theatre has a good-value
café with an adjoining restaurant and
terrace area. Perfect for enjoying a
meal before a show.

Sushi at The Tatami Room

6 The Tatami Room
MAP C4 ▪ C/Poeta Cabanyes 19
▪ 93 329 67 40 ▪ Closed Mon ▪ €

Modelled on a traditional Japanese
inn, this eatery has a wide variety
of well-prepared Japanese dishes,
from sushi to curries and noodles.

7 La Federica
MAP D4 ▪ C/de Salvà 3
▪ 93 600 59 01 ▪ Closed Sun &
Mon ▪ €

This funky, vintage-style bar serves
a fantastic brunch, as well as tasty
and imaginative tapas to go with
its good range of cocktails.

8 Malamen
MAP C4 ▪ C/Blai 53
▪ 93 252 77 63 ▪ Closed Mon ▪ €

This hipster favourite serves gourmet
tapas accompanied by an extensive
and carefully chosen wine selection
in ultra-stylish surroundings.

9 Restaurant Forestier
MAP C5 ▪ Pl Carlos Ibáñez 3
▪ 93 281 16 00 ▪ €€

This elegant restaurant in the Hotel
Miramar has amazing views.

10 Quimet & Quimet
MAP C4 ▪ C/Poeta Cabanyes
25 ▪ 93 442 31 42 ▪ Closed Sat eve,
Sun, Aug ▪ €

This tiny bodega has standing room
only, but serves delicious tapas and
wonderful wines.

PRICE CATEGORIES

For a three-course meal for one with half
a bottle of wine (or equivalent meal),
including taxes and extra charges.

€ under €35   €€ €35–50   €€€ over €50

See map on p94 ←

🔟 The Seafront

The heady allure of the Mediterranean permeates the city and a dip into its azure waters is only ever a few metro stops away. The city's beaches were once hidden behind an industrial wasteland, but things changed radically in preparation for the 1992 Olympics. The plan was to create a city *oberta al mar* (open to the sea); the result is phenomenal. Tons of sand were transported to create miles of beaches from Barceloneta to Port Olímpic and beyond. Palm trees were planted, water cleanliness standards implemented and contemporary sculptures erected. Nearby Port Olímpic

Monument a Colom

now throbs with scores of bars, clubs and restaurants, while a section of Poblenou, designated 22@Barcelona by a city council keen to bring in new technological and design business, has been transformed over the last decade.

THE SEAFRONT

1 Museu d'Història de Catalunya

MAP N6 ■ Pl Pau Vila 3 ■ Open 10am–7pm Tue–Sat (to 8pm Wed), 10am–2:30pm Sun ■ Adm; free last Tue of the month (Oct–Jun) ■ www. mhcat.cat

Housed in the Palau de Mar, a renovated portside warehouse, this museum offers a broad, interactive exploration of Catalonia's history since prehistoric times *(see p53)*. Kids especially will have a ball with the engaging exhibits, such as a Civil War-era bunker and a recreated Catalan bar from the 1960s with an ancient *futbolín* (table football) game.

2 Rambla de Mar

MAP E5 ■ Moll d'Espanya ■ Maremagnum: shops 10am–10pm daily, restaurants until 1am daily

Saunter along the Rambla de Mar, a floating wooden pier that leads to the flashy Maremagnum mall.

The floating Rambla de Mar pier

It is open every day of the year, which makes it particularly popular with shoppers on Sundays.

3 Beaches

MAP E6

If you fancy a splash in the Mediterranean, head down to the end of La Rambla, wander along the palm tree-lined Moll de la Fusta, and down the restaurant-packed Passeig Joan de Borbó where the sea beckons. More than 4 km (2.5 miles) of blue-flag beaches stretch north from Barceloneta to Port Olímpic and beyond. Facilities are top-notch, including showers, deck chairs, beach volleyball courts and life-guards. Convenience, however, means crowds, so finding a spot among the masses of oiled bodies can be a challenge, particularly during the summer.

4 L'Aquàrium de Barcelona

MAP E6 ■ Moll d'Espanya ■ Open from 10am daily; closing times vary from 7:30pm to 9:30pm depending on month and day ■ Adm ■ www.aquariumbcn.com/en

Come face to face with the marine world of the Mediterranean at the largest aquarium in Europe. The highlight is an 80-m- (262-ft-) long underwater tunnel, with a moving walkway that transports you through the deep blue, while sharks glide menacingly close. A huge hit with the kids is the Explora! floor, where interactive exhibits allow you to experience the ecosystems of the Mediterranean *(see p52)*.

Old buildings of Barceloneta

5 Barceloneta
MAP F5

A portside warren of narrow streets, small squares and ancient bars, this traditional neighbourhood of *pescadors* (fishermen) and *mariners* (sailors) seems worlds apart from the mega-malls and disco lights of nearby Port Olímpic. A refreshing foray through this tight-knit community yields a glimpse into the Barcelona of 150 years ago. Older couples still pull chairs out onto the street to gossip and watch the world go by, and small seafood restaurants serve a *menú del dia* of whatever is fresh off the boat. Running the length of Barceloneta's western edge is the Passeig Joan de Borbó, which is lined with restaurants serving *mariscs* (shellfish) and paellas.

6 Pailebot Santa Eulàlia
MAP L6 ■ Moll de la Fusta
■ Open Apr–Oct: 10am–8:30pm Tue–Sat; Nov–Mar: 10am–5:30pm Tue–Sun ■ Adm

Bobbing in the water at the Moll de la Fusta (Timber Quay) is this restored three-mast schooner, originally christened *Carmen Flores*. It first set sail from Spain in 1918. On journeys to Cuba, the ship used to transport textiles and salt, returning with tobacco, coffee, cereals and wood. In 1997, the Museu Marítim *(see p87)* bought and restored the ship as part of a project to create a collection of seaworthy historical Catalan vessels.

7 Boat and Cable-Car Trips
MAP E5/6 ■ Telefèric: from Torre San Sebastià ■ Las Golondrinas: Portal de la Pau ■ Approximately every 30 mins from 11:30am ■ www.lasgolondrinas. com ■ Orsom: Portal de la Pau ■ For timings call 93 441 05 37 ■ www. barcelona-orsom.com

Observe all the activity at Barcelona's bustling port area from a different perspective, either from the air or the sea. The *Transbordador Aeri* cable cars offer sweeping bird's-eye views of Barcelona and its coast, while the old-fashioned Las Golondrinas "swallow boats" and the Orsom Catamaran make regular sightseeing trips around the harbour, the beaches and the port area.

8 Monument a Colom
MAP E5

This 60-m- (197-ft-) high column was built between 1882 and 1888 for Barcelona's Universal Exhibition and commemorates Christopher Columbus's first voyage to the Americas – it was in Barcelona that Columbus met Ferdinand and Isabel on his return. Columbus himself stands proudly on top of the column, pointing out to sea, supposedly towards the New World but actually towards Italy. A lift swooshes up the column to a viewing platform located just below Columbus's feet, which offers fabulous 360° views *(see p16)*.

9 Poblenou and Palo Alto Design Complex

MAP H5 ■ www.poblenouurbandistrict. com/en ■ www.paloaltobcn.org

The increasingly fashionable Poblenou district is home to a burgeoning number of trendy cafés and shops, as well as old industrial warehouses and buildings that are being restored and repurposed. One contains BD Design, the city's most prestigious design showroom, while the Palo Alto complex houses the studios of big-name designers. It also hosts popular craft and design markets one weekend a month.

10 Museu Blau

Pl Leonardo da Vinci 4–5, Parc del Fórum ■ 93 256 60 02 ■ Open Oct–Feb: 10am–6pm Tue–Fri (to 7pm Sat, to 8pm Sun & hols); Mar–Sep: 10am–7pm Tue–Sat (to 8pm Sun & hols) ■ Adm; free first Sun of the month, every Sun after 3pm ■ www.museuciencies.cat

The Blue Museum, the main site of the Museu de Ciències Naturals, occupies a raised triangular building constructed by Herzog & de Meuron for Barcelona's Forum 2004 event. This is a great, family-friendly place, with an appealing mix of contemporary exhibits and wonderfully old-fashioned cabinets full of stuffed animals. The main exhibition is a "biography of the earth", with interactive audio-visual displays about the origins of the world. There is a special area for the under-7s to learn about science, plus a library and café.

Museu Blau

EXPLORING THE PORT

▶ MORNING

Begin your port *passeig* (stroll) with a visit to the **Museu Marítim** *(see p87)*, where you can sense Barcelona's status as one of the most active ports in the Mediterranean. From here, head towards the Monument a Colom and stroll along the Moll de la Fusta to admire the **Pailebot Santa Eulàlia**, which has been immaculately restored by the museum. Saunter down the **Rambla de Mar** *(see p101)*, an undulating wooden drawbridge that leads to the **Maremagnum** mega-mall. At the start of the pier, take a boat ride on the **Orsom Catamaran**, where you can grab a drink and a snack. Soak up the sunshine and the port skyline while sprawled out on a net just inches above the water. Back on land, stroll down the Moll d'Espanya and turn towards the traditional fisher-man's quarter of **Barceloneta**, an atmospheric pocket of narrow streets and timeworn bars. Get a real taste of old-style Barcelona at the boisterous tapas place, **El Vaso de Oro** (C/Balboa 6). Wedge yourself in at the bar and savour some tasty seafood morsels.

AFTERNOON

Head to Passeig Joan de Borbó and the beach. Douse yourself in the Med, then siesta in the afternoon sun. Pick yourself up with sangria at the beachside **Salamanca** *xiringuito* (at the end of Pg Joan de Borbó), where you can bury your feet in the sand and watch the waves lap the shore as the sun dips below the horizon.

See map on pp100–101 ←

Bars and Beach Clubs

Pleasant outdoor seating at Boo

1 Boo
Espigó de Bac de Roda 1, Platja Nova Mar Bella ▪ 93 225 01 00
This restaurant, cocktail lounge and beach club offers drinks, tapas, live music and DJ sessions.

2 CDLC
MAP G6 ▪ Pg Marítim de la Barceloneta 32
Right by the beach, with a terrace to relax on, this is a restaurant that becomes a club after dinner. Guest DJs feature every week.

3 Bar Jai Ca
MAP F5 ▪ C/Ginebra 13 ▪ 93 268 32 65 ▪ Closed Mon
The television blares and kids race around in this relaxed neighbourhood favourite. Delicious tapas and good wine are on offer.

4 Club Catwalk
MAP G6 ▪ Ramón Trías Fargas 2–4 ▪ Adm ▪ clubcatwalk.net
One of the hottest clubs in town, this has two floors – one for chilling out, the other for dancing to techno, deep house or mainstream sounds – along with a terrace bar.

5 Shôko
MAP E6 ▪ Pg Marítim de la Barceloneta 36
Doubling as a Japanese restaurant during the day, this club by the beach provides all kinds of music in a great setting. Can get very crowded.

6 Xiringuito Escribà
Av Litoral 62, Platja de Bogatell ▪ 93 221 07 29
A beach bar right on the sand open for breakfast, tapas, light meals and excellent cocktails made with fresh fruits and premium spirits.

7 Mar Bella beach bars
Platja Nova Mar Bella ▪ Open summer only
Head to one of the *xiringuitos* (beach bars) on Barcelona's hippest beach and enjoy the DJ sessions.

8 Eclipse
MAP F6 ▪ W Hotel, Pl de la Rosa dels Vents 1 ▪ 93 295 28 00
The spectacular bar on the 26th floor of the W Hotel (commonly known as the Hotel Vela) offers magnificent views of the city. Smart dress code.

The opulent poolside club Arola

9 Arola
MAP G5 ▪ Hotel Arts, C/Marina 19–21 ▪ 93 483 80 90 ▪ Open Thu–Mon
A luxurious, summer-only poolside bar at the plush Hotel Arts, the Arola has huge white beds covered with silk cushions, DJ sessions, and a range of perfectly-mixed cocktails.

10 Razzmatazz
MAP H4 ▪ C/Almogàvers 122 (The Loft: C/Pamplona 88) ▪ Razz Club and Loft closed Sun–Tue
Concerts, from rock to jazz, feature several nights a week at this trendy club, which has five spaces offering a range of musical styles, including the Razz Club and the Loft *(see p59)*.

Restaurants and Tapas Bars

PRICE CATEGORIES

For a three-course meal for one with half a bottle of wine (or equivalent meal), including taxes and extra charges.

€ under €35 €€ €35–50 €€€ over €50

1 Set Portes
MAP N5 ▪ Pg Isabel II 14
▪ 93 319 30 33 ▪ €€

Founded in 1836, this legendary city institution serves some of the finest Catalan cuisine in the city, including a variety of paellas.

2 Segons Mercat
MAP F5 & Q6 ▪ C/Balboa 16 ▪ 93 310 78 80 ▪ Open daily 1–4:30pm & 8–11:30pm, all day in summer ▪ €

Tuck into tasty tapas from grilled cuttlefish to *patates braves* at this stylish, modern spot, which also serves more substantial rice and seafood dishes.

3 Green Spot
MAP P5 ▪ C/Reina Cristina 12 ▪ 93 802 55 65 ▪ €€

A spacious restaurant with sleek, minimalist design, serving some of the best vegetarian and vegan food in the city.

4 Somorrostro

MAP F6 ▪ C/Sant Carles 11 ▪ 93 225 00 10 ▪ Open 1pm–midnight daily ▪ €

This chic restaurant serves a daily changing Catalan menu prepared with fresh ingredients. Relaxed ambience and decor.

5 La Bombeta

MAP F6 ▪ C/Maquinista 33 ▪ 93 319 94 45 ▪ Closed Wed ▪ €

This traditional Catalan bar, very popular with locals, offers a wonderful glimpse of life in Barcelona before the tourists arrived. The house speciality is the *bombas*, deep-fried balls of mashed potatoes served with a spicy tomato sauce.

6 Salamanca

MAP F6 ▪ C/Almirall Cervera 34 ▪ 93 221 50 33 ▪ €€

This may feel like a tourist trap at first, but the food is top notch. There are plenty of meat dishes on offer.

7 Can Ganassa
MAP F6 ▪ Pl de la Barceloneta 4–6 ▪ 93 252 84 49 ▪ €

An old-style, family-run tapas bar that has been serving fresh seafood tapas to locals for decades.

8 Kaiku
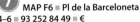
MAP E6 ▪ Pl del Mar 1 ▪ 93 221 90 82 ▪ Closed Sun eve in winter, Mon ▪ €€

Decorated with fishing nets, Kaiku *(see p62)* is known for seafood, especially the *arros del xef* (chef's rice).

9 Suquet de l'Almirall
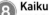
MAP F6 ▪ Pg Joan de Borbó 65 ▪ 93 221 62 33 ▪ Closed Sun eve, Mon (except eve Apr–Sep), lunch in Aug ▪ €€

This family-run gem serves excellent *arroz de barca* (rice in broth, with seafood) and *suquet* (seafood and potato stew).

10 La Mar Salada
MAP E6 ▪ Pg de Joan de Borbó 58 ▪ 93 221 21 27 ▪ Closed Tue ▪ €€

This light, bright restaurant near the sea serves modern fare with an emphasis on seafood, including monkfish with wild mushrooms and artichokes, and paella. The weekday set lunch menu is great value.

Tàrtar de sorell at La Mar Salada

See map on pp100–101

🔟 Eixample

If the old town is the heart of Barcelona and green Tibidabo and Montjuïc its lungs, the Eixample is its nervous system – its economic and commercial core. The area took shape in 1860, when the city was allowed to expand beyond the medieval walls. Based on plans by Catalan engineer Ildefons Cerdà, the Eixample is laid out on a grid. Construction continued into the 20th century at a time when the elite was patronizing the most daring architects. *Modernisme* was flourishing and the area became home to the best of Barcelona's

Rooftop, La Pedrera

Modernista architecture, with its elegant façades and balconies. Today, enchanting cafés, funky design shops, gourmet restaurants and hip bars draw the professional crowd, which has adopted the neighbourhood as its own.

EIXAMPLE

- **1** Top 10 Sights *see pp106–9*
- **1** Restaurants and Tapas Bars *see p113*
- **1** Design Shops *see p110*
- **1** After-Dark Venues *see p111*
- **1** Cafés *see p112*

① Sagrada Família
Gaudí's wizardry culminated in this enchanting, wild, unconventional church, which dominates the city skyline (see pp12–15).

② La Pedrera
A daring, surreal fantasyland, and Gaudí's most remarkable civic work (see pp26–7).

③ Sant Pau Recinte Modernista
MAP H1 ■ C/Sant Antoni Maria Claret 167 ■ 93 553 78 11 ■ Open Apr–Oct: 10am–6:30pm Mon–Sat (Nov–Mar: to 4:30pm), 10am–2:30pm Sun ■ Adm; guided tours in English 11am daily ■ www.santpaubarcelona.org
Founded in 1401, the Hospital de la Santa Creu i de Sant Pau was a fully-functioning hospital until 2009, when all medical activities were moved to a new building and the UNESCO World Heritage Site exquisitely

Sant Pau Recinte Modernista

restored and opened to the public (see pp44–5). The Art Nouveau site, created by Domènech i Montaner between 1902 and 1930, is a tribute to *Modernisme* – and Domènech's answer to Gaudí's Sagrada Família. There are eight pavilions, which recall the history of Catalonia using murals, mosaics and sculptures, and various other buildings, all linked by underground tunnels. The buildings are interlaced by beautiful gardens and courtyards. The site is part of the Ruta del Modernisme (see p140).

④ Mansana de la Discòrdia
MAP E2 ■ Pg de Gràcia 35–45
At the heart of the city's *Quadrat d'Or* (Golden Square) lies this stunning row of houses. The "block of discord" is so named because of the dramatic contrast between its three flagship buildings. Built between 1900 and 1907 by the three *Modernista* greats, rival architects Gaudí, Domènech i Montaner and Puig i Cadafalch, the houses were commissioned by competing bourgeois families. Domènech is represented by the ornate Casa Lleó Morera (see p45), Puig by the Gothic-inspired Casa Amatller (see p45), and Gaudí by the whimsical Casa Batlló (see p45). Among them, the Casa Amatller and Casa Batlló can be toured. The houses at Nos. 37 and 39 add to the splendour of the block. At No. 39 is the Museu del Perfum (see p43).

The Els Encants market space

6 Els Encants

MAP H3 ▪ Av Meridiana 69 ▪ 92 246 30 30 ▪ Open 9am–8pm Mon, Wed, Fri, Sat ▪ www.encantsbcn.com

For almost a hundred years, the Els Encants market was a rambling, chaotic jumble of street stalls. In 2014 it got a striking new home and now its stalls are arranged in a gentle upward spiral under a mirrored, angled canopy designed to keep off the sun. As well as antiques, bric-a-brac and plain old junk, you'll find textiles, household goods, records and vintage clothes here (see p68).

7 Casa Terrades – "Casa de les Punxes"

MAP F2 ▪ Av Diagonal 416 ▪ Guided tours 9am–8pm daily ▪ Adm ▪ www.casadelespunxes.com

This Gothic-style castle with four towers was designed by the *Modernista* architect Josep Puig i Cadafalch and finished in 1905 for the Terrades sisters. It has always housed private homes. From the outside you can admire the forged ironwork on the balconies, the carved reliefs and the colourful stained-glass windows. The ceramic panels mounted on the façade represent the patriotic symbols of Catalonia.

Cloud and Chair, **Fundació Tàpies**

5 Fundació Tàpies

MAP E2 ▪ C/Aragó 255 ▪ 93 487 03 15 ▪ Open 10am–7pm Tue–Sun ▪ Adm (free under 16) ▪ www.fundaciotapies.org

Paintings and sculptures by Antoni Tàpies (1923–2012), who was Catalonia's foremost artist, are housed in this early *Modernista* building (see p32). For a glimpse of what awaits inside, look up – crowning the museum is the artist's eye-catching wire sculpture *Cloud and Chair* (1990). The collection of over 300 pieces covers Tàpies' whole range of work, including impressive abstract pieces such as *Grey Ochre on Brown* (1962). Temporary exhibitions are also held here, with past shows by Mario Herz and Hans Hacke.

8 Rambla de Catalunya
MAP E2

This elegant extension of the better-known Rambla is a more upmarket version. Lined with trees that form a leafy green tunnel in summer, it boasts scores of pretty façades and shops, including the *Modernista* Farmàcia Bolos (No. 77). The avenue teems with terrace bars and cafés (*see pp66–7*).

9 Museu Egipci
MAP E2 ▪ C/València 284 ▪ 93 488 01 88 ▪ Open 10am–8pm Mon–Sat (closed 2–4pm Jan to mid-June & early Sep–Nov); 10am–2pm Sun ▪ Adm ▪ www.museuegipci.com

Spain's most important Egyptology museum houses more than 350 exhibits from over 3,000 years of Ancient Egyptian history. Exhibits include terracotta figures, human and animal mummies, and a bust of the goddess Sekhmet (700–300 BC).

10 Museu del Disseny de Barcelona
MAP H3 ▪ Pl de la Glòries Catalanes 37–38 ▪ 93 256 68 00 ▪ Open 10am–8pm Tue–Sun ▪ ajuntament.barcelona.cat/museudeldisseny

A monolithic hulk hosts this museum showcasing archirecure, fashion, product and graphic design. It also houses two leading independent, non-profit associations promoting design and architecture, the Foment de les Arts i del Disseny (FAD) (*see p87*) and Barcelona Centre de Disseny (BCD).

Disseny Museum

THE MODERNISTA ROUTE

▶ MORNING

Visit the **Museu del Modernisme de Barcelona** (*C/Balmes 48, www.mmbcn.cat*) for an introduction to Catalan Art Nouveau via a series of fascinating temporary exhibitions, then stroll around the gardens of the university. Head east along Gran Via past the elegant **El Palace Barcelona Hotel** (*see p143*) and turn right down C/Bruc and right again onto C/Casp for a glimpse of Gaudí's **Casa Calvet** (*see p113*). Walk two blocks west to the majestic Pg de Gràcia; then go right again three blocks to the **Mansana de la Discòrdia** (*see p107*) and explore Casa Lleó Morera, Casa Amatller or Casa Batlló – or all three if you have the time and energy. Sniff around the **Museu del Perfum** (*see p43*) and **Regia** perfume shop (*see p110*) before continuing north to marvel at Gaudí's **La Pedrera** (*see pp26–7*). Take a lunch break at **Windsor** (*see p113*). Their set menu is an enjoyable way to experience Catalan *haute cuisine*.

AFTERNOON

After lunch, return to Pg de Gràcia then turn right along Av Diagonal, taking in the fairy-tale **Casa de les Punxes** at No. 416 (*see p45*). Continue on Diagonal, turning left at Pg Sant Joan to see the exhibition on Modernism in the **Palau Macaya** at No. 108. Then stroll along C/Mallorca to the **Sagrada Família** (*see pp12–15*). Here you can take in the Nativity Façade and rest weary legs in the Plaça de Gaudí before climbing the bell towers for a breathtaking view of the city.

See map on pp106–7 ←

Design Shops

A dazzling display at Pilma

1 Pilma
MAP E1 ■ Av Diagonal 403

A stunning shop selling quality modern furniture and interior accessories by big names, as well as cutting-edge creations by a range of Catalan designers.

2 L'Appartement
MAP E2 ■ C/Enric Granados 44
■ Closed Sun

A spacious, white-painted store packed to the rafters with gorgeous furnishings and knick-knacks at reasonable prices – from quirky, cool lights and sculptures to bags, jewellery and T-shirts.

3 Regia
MAP E2 ■ Pg de Gràcia 39

The biggest perfume shop in the city has over 1,000 scents to choose from, including all the leading brands, and smaller makers. The space also plays host to the Museu del Perfum (see p43).

4 Dos i Una
MAP E2 ■ C/Rosselló 275

A designer gift shop with a steel-tiled floor and psychedelic colour scheme. Concentrates on selling "made in Barcelona" items, which make for unusual souvenirs.

5 Ultima Parada
MAP E2 ■ C/Rosselló 271
■ Closed Sun

A retro shop run by photographers Bela Adler and Salvador Fresneda, who recycle industrial 1950s, 70s and 80s objects and furniture.

6 Nanimarquina
MAP F2 ■ Rosselló 256

Exquisite handmade carpets and textiles are displayed in this artful, whitewashed showroom.

7 Azultierra
MAP E2 ■ C/Corsega 276–282
■ Closed Sun

A huge, warehouse-style space with exquisite furniture as well as lighting and all kinds of decorative objects ranging from mirrors to candles.

8 DBarcelona
MAP F2 ■ Av Diagonal 367

An eclectic range of gadgets and gifts in a shop that doubles as an exhibition space for up-and-coming designers and established artists.

9 Jaime Beriestain
MAP E2 ■ C/Pau Claris 167
■ 93 515 07 79

The celebrated Chilean designer's concept store offers gorgeous houseware – light fixtures, kitchenware, tableware, furnishings and furniture – as well as gourmet food items, books, cards and knick-knacks. It also boasts a spectacularly stylish café and restaurant that is open all week until late.

Kitchenware by Jaime Beriestain

10 Bagués Joieria
MAP E2 ■ Pg de Gràcia 41
■ Closed Sun

Every piece on sale at this renowned jewellery shop, which was established in 1839, is handmade using traditional methods.

After-Dark Venues

1 Milano
MAP E3 ▪ Ronda Universitat 35 ▪ Open noon–2:30am daily

Red velvet sofas and expertly mixed cocktails make this a great option for late-night drinks. There are periodic live jazz performances (see p59).

2 Xixbar
MAP C4 ▪ C/Rocafort 19

A small bar with a big reputation. The gin and tonics, prepared with a range of gins sold in the shop next door, are considered the city's best.

3 Les Gens que j'Aime
MAP E2 ▪ C/Valencia 286 ▪ Open 6pm–2:30am daily (to 3am weekends)

The ideal place to have a drink and enjoy lounge music after exploring the area around Passeig de Gràcia and Rambla Catalunya.

4 Slow Bar
MAP D1 ▪ C/Paris 186

This red-hued cocktail bar also has a club and live music venue. It offers a wide range of finely mixed cocktails.

5 Bar Marfil
MAP E2 ▪ Rambla de Catalunya 104

Part of the Hotel Murmuri, this is a trendy bar on a fancy shopping street. Sink into a plush faux-Baroque armchair and sip a delectable cocktail.

6 Luz de Gas
MAP D1 ▪ C/Muntaner 246

A classic late-night watering hole, this place is half concert hall, half bar. It has live music nightly, from blues to jazz and soul.

7 Ideal
MAP D2 ▪ C/Aribau 89 ▪ Closed Sun

Luxurious cocktail lounge opened by legendary barman José María Gotarda in 1931 and now run by his son. More than 80 varieties of whisky.

8 City Hall
MAP E3 ▪ Rambla de Catalunya 2–4 ▪ Closed Mon

This popular club has two dance floors. Club nights cover a range of music styles, from electro pop to drum 'n' bass.

9 Ajoblanco
MAP E1 ▪ C/Tuset 20 ▪ Open daily until 3am

This swish eatery turns into a hotspot for cocktails late in the evening, with live music on Wednesdays and DJs on the weekends. The drinks list also features great local wines.

10 Dry Martini
MAP D2 ▪ C/Aribau 162

A classic and elegant venue where extraordinarily talented bartenders are ready to prepare your favourite cocktail. Jazz plays unobtrusively in the background.

Bar area at Dry Martini

See map on pp106–7

Cafés

Gallery café Galeria Cosmo is decorated with artworks

 Laie Llibreria Cafè
MAP E3 ■ C/Pau Claris 85
■ Closed Sun

A cultural meeting place with a lively atmosphere, airy terrace and one of the best bookshops in town. There's an excellent set lunch *(see p64)*.

 Cafè del Centre
MAP F3 ■ C/Girona 69
■ Closed Sun

Said to be the oldest café in the Eixample, with dark wooden interiors that have not changed for a century, this is an unpretentious spot for a quiet coffee.

③ **Casa Alfonso**
MAP F3 ■ C/Roger de Llúria 6
■ Closed Sun

This classy café has been in business since 1929. Arguably the best *pernil* (serrano ham) in the city.

④ **Cacao Sampaka**
MAP E3 ■ C/Consell de Cent 292 ■ Closed Sun

An infinite array of chocolate, including innovative combinations such as chocolate with Parmesan cheese or olive oil.

⑤ **Pastelerias Mauri**
MAP E2 ■ Rambla Catalunya 102 ■ Closed Sun from 3pm

One of the best pastry shops in town ever since its opening in 1929. Enjoy a hot drink with an elaborate dessert in *Modernista* surroundings.

⑥ **Galeria Cosmo**
MAP E2 ■ C/Enric Granados 3
■ Open 10am–10pm Mon & Tue, 10am–11pm Wed & Thu, 10am–midnight Fri & Sat, 11am–10pm Sun

This art gallery café on a semi-pedestrianized street offers sandwiches, cakes and tapas.

⑦ **Cornelia & Co.**
MAP E2 ■ C/Valencia 225

Come to this great spot near the Passeig de Gràcia for brunch, coffee, cake, a light meal, or just pop in to pick up some deli goodies.

⑧ **Velódromo**
MAP D1 ■ C/Muntaner 213
■ 93 430 60 22

This historic bar with original 1930s furnishings was reopened by local celebrity chef Charles Abellan. The menu features sophisticated versions of Catalan classics.

⑨ **Manso's Café**
MAP C4 ■ C/Manso 1
■ Closed Mon

Enjoy fabulous homemade cakes, great coffee (with a choice of milks), delicious soups and quiches at this café. Dine on the little terrace or in the cosy interior.

⑩ **Joséphine**
MAP E2 ■ C/Pau Claris 147

Coffee and snacks are served all day at this French colonial café. There's also an evening menu.

Restaurants and Tapas Bars

PRICE CATEGORIES
For a three-course meal for one with half a bottle of wine (or equivalent meal), including taxes and extra charges.

€ under €35　€€ €35–50　€€€ over €50

1 **Monvínic**
MAP E3 ▪ C/Diputació 249 ▪ 93 272 61 87 ▪ Closed Sun, Mon & lunch Sat ▪ €€

An ultra-trendy wine bar with a global wine list. They have excellent tapas plus more substantial fare.

2 **Cinc Sentits**
MAP D2 ▪ C/Aribau 58 ▪ 93 323 94 90 ▪ Closed Sun & Mon ▪ €€€

Indulge the five senses (cinc sentits in Catalan) at this stylish restaurant where the chef's contemporary interpretations of classic Catalan cuisine have won it a Michelin star (see p63).

3 **Igueldo**
MAP E2 ▪ C/Rosselló 186 ▪ 93 452 25 55 ▪ Closed Sun ▪ €€

Updated Basque cuisine is served in elegant surroundings, and there's a tapas counter too (see p62).

4 **Casa Calvet**
MAP F3 ▪ C/Casp 48 ▪ 93 412 40 12 ▪ Closed Sun & public hols ▪ €€

Catalan food with a modern twist is served in beautifully-designed dining rooms by Gaudí.

5 **Roca Moo**
MAP E2 ▪ C/Rosselló 265 ▪ 93 445 40 00 ▪ Closed Sun, Mon, 2 weeks in Jan, 2 weeks in Aug ▪ €€€

Overseen by the Roca brothers, Moo in Hotel Omm (see pp142–3) serves creative Catalan fare and boasts a Michelin star. Book in advance.

6 **Cervecería Catalana**
MAP E2 ▪ C/Mallorca 236 ▪ 93 216 03 68 ▪ €

Some of the best tapas in town served with a variety of beers, close to the Rambla de Catalunya.

7 **Windsor**
MAP E1 ▪ C/Còrsega 286 ▪ 93 237 75 88 ▪ Closed 3 weeks in Aug ▪ €€€

Catalan *haute cuisine* is served in elegant surroundings with chandeliers and red upholstered furniture. There's also a garden for alfresco dining (see p62).

8 **La Taverna del Clínic**
MAP D2 ▪ C/Rosselló 155 ▪ 93 410 42 21 ▪ Closed Sun ▪ €€

This bar looks ordinary on the outside, but its excellent, contemporary tapas is among the best in the city (see p62).

9 **Paco Meralgo**
MAP D1 ▪ C/Muntaner 171 ▪ 93 430 90 27 ▪ €

This bright, stylish tapas bar has a gourmet menu based on recipes from around the country.

10 **Moments**
MAP E3 ▪ Pg de Gràcia 38–40 ▪ 93 151 87 81 ▪ Closed Sun & Mon ▪ €€€

Set in the ultra-luxurious Mandarin Oriental (see p145), Moments has been awarded two Michelin stars for its sublime renditions of Catalan classics, from langoustine tartare to scallops with artichokes. A la carte and tasting menus offered.

Moments at the Mandarin Oriental

See map on pp106–7 ←

TOP10 Gràcia, Tibidabo and Zona Alta

The hilly Zona Alta covers several neighbourhoods, from the moneyed Pedralbes and Tibidabo to bohemian Gràcia. The area offers stunning views and regal attractions, but what sets it apart are its 15 parks – the best are Collserola, spread like green baize over Tibidabo mountain, and Gaudí's Parc Güell. Cosmopolitan Gràcia's political tradition and gypsy community have long drawn artists and writers to its labyrinthine streets, and its squares are now home to lively bars and stores.

Torre de Collserola

GRÀCIA, TIBIDABO AND ZONA ALTA

- **1** Top 10 Sights *see pp116–19*
- **①** Restaurants and Tapas Bars *see p123*
- **①** Gràcia Boutiques *see p120*
- **①** Hip Drinking Spots *see p122*
- **①** Gràcia Cafés *see p121*

1 Monestir de Pedralbes

MAP A1 ■ C/Baixada del Monestir 9 ■ Open Apr–Sep: 10am–5pm Tue–Fri (to 7pm Sat, to 8pm Sun); Oct–Mar: 10am–2pm Tue–Fri (to 5pm Sat & Sun) ■ Adm; free first Sun of the month, every Sun 3–8pm) ■ www.monestir pedralbes.bcn.cat

Named after the Latin *petras albas*, which means "white stones", this outstandingly beautiful Gothic monastery *(see p40)* was founded by Queen Elisenda de Montcada de Piños in 1327 with the support of her husband James II of Aragón. Her alabaster tomb lies in the wall between the church and the impressive three-storey Gothic cloister. The furnished kitchens, cells, infirmary

Monestir de Pedralbes

and refectory, which are all well preserved, provide an interesting glimpse into medieval life.

2 Parc d'Atraccions del Tibidabo

MAP B1 ■ Pl de Tibidabo ■ Opening times vary, check website ■ Adm ■ www.tibidabo.cat

Take the funicular up to the top of Tibidabo's 517-m (1,695-ft) mountain to visit this traditional amusement park, which opened in 1908 *(see p52)*. There are a couple of white-knuckle rides, but the real attractions are the old-fashioned ones, including a beautifully-preserved carousel and a Ferris wheel. There's also the Museu dels Autòmates *(see p43)*, with automatons, mechanical models and a scale model of the park.

3 Torre de Collserola

MAP B1 ■ Parc de Collserola ■ Opening times vary, check website ■ Adm ■ www.torrede collserola.com

This slender telecommunications tower was designed by British architect Sir Norman Foster. The needle-like upper structure rests on a concrete pillar, anchored by 12 huge steel cables. Rising to a height of 288 m (945 ft), the top is reached by a glass-fronted lift. On a clear day, you can see Montserrat and the Pyrenees.

Camp Nou, FC Barcelona's home stadium

4 Camp Nou Experience

MAP A2 ▪ Entrance 9 Stadium, Av Arístides Maillol ▪ Opening times vary, check website; advance booking recommended ▪ Adm ▪ www.fcbarcelona.com/camp-nou

The Museu del FC Barcelona (see p42), Barcelona's most visited museum, is a must for fans of the beautiful game. Numerous displays of football memorabilia show all you need to know about the club. Work donated by some of Catalonia's leading artists is also on display. Admission includes access to Barca's 120,000-seater stadium, Camp Nou, an impressive monument to the city's love affair with the game.

5 CosmoCaixa Museu de la Ciència

MAP B1 ▪ C/Isaac Newton 26 ▪ 93 212 60 50 ▪ Open 10am–8pm Tue–Sun (summer & Christmas: also Mon) ▪ Adm (free under 16)

Barcelona's science museum is a thoroughly stimulating and interactive affair. It occupies a glass-and-steel building, with six of its nine storeys set underground. Displays include a wide range of historic objects, flora and fauna. One of its most important pieces is a recreated section of flooded Amazon rainforest, including fish, reptiles, mammals, birds and plants. A tour through Earth's geological history explains processes such as erosion and sedimentation. There are also innovative temporary exhibitions on environmental issues (see p43).

6 Parc Güell

A UNESCO World Heritage Site, this heady brew of architectural wizardry (see pp22–3) includes trencadís tiling, fairy-tale pavilions, Gothic archways and the columned Sala Hipóstila (originally designed as a market hall). In true Gaudí style, playfulness and symbolism pervade every aspect of the park. The Casa-Museu Gaudí, where Gaudí lived for 20 years, is dedicated to his life.

7 Parc del Laberint d'Horta

MAP C1 ▪ C/German Desvalls ▪ Open 10am–dusk daily ▪ Adm; free Wed, Sun & Mar–mid-Aug

In 1802, the Marquès d'Alfarràs hosted a huge party in these wonderful Neo-Classical gardens to celebrate the visit of Charles IV. Designed by the Italian architect Domenico Bagutti, they incorporate pavilions, a lake, a waterfall, canals and a cypress-tree hedge maze.

GRÀCIA

Until the late 19th century, Gràcia was a fiercely proud independent city. Despite locals' protests, it became part of Barcelona proper in 1898, but has always maintained a sense of separatism and has been a hotbed of political activity. It is now home to a booming cottage industry nurtured by a growing band of artisans. Don't miss the *barri*'s annual fiesta (see p72) in the second week of August.

8 Parc de Collserola
MAP B1 ∎ Info point:
C/Església 92 ∎ 93 280 35 52
∎ www.parcnaturalcollserola.cat

Beyond the peaks of Tibidabo mountain, this 6,500-ha (16,000-acre) natural park of wild forest and winding paths is an oasis of calm. It is great for hiking and biking, with signposted paths and nature trails.

9 Tramvia Blau
MAP B1 ∎ Av Tibidabo
∎ Trams run Easter, mid-Jun–mid-Sep: 10am–7:30pm daily; rest of year: 10am–7:30pm Sat & Sun (end Oct–mid-Mar: to 6pm) ∎ Adm

The city's blue trams, with their charmingly old-fashioned wooden interiors are attractions in their own right. The route, from the FGC station to Plaça Doctor Andreu passes many *Modernista* mansions to the top of Avinguda Tibidabo.

10 Temple Expiatori del Sagrat Cor

Visible from almost anywhere in Barcelona, the Neo-Gothic Temple of the Sacred Heart (see p40) was built by Enric Sagnier between 1902 and 1911. It has a dramatic sculpture of Jesus on top of the structure, and an elaborately decorated door. Take the elevator up the main tower, or climb the steps to the outside terrace for breathtaking views.

Temple Expiatori del Sagrat Cor

EXPLORING THE HEIGHTS

▶ MORNING

Taking the northern route of the Bus Turístic (see p140) is the easiest way to negotiate the vast northern area of the city; it also gives discounts on entrance to major sights en route. Start off at Plaça de Catalunya (tickets can be bought on board) and sit on the top deck for a good view of the *Modernista* magic along Pg de Gràcia. Make the whimsical **Parc Güell** your first stop and spend the morning ambling around Gaudí's otherworldly park. Get back on the bus and continue north to the southern end of Av Tibidabo. Walk about 500 m (1,600 ft) up Av Tibidabo and stop off for a leisurely lunch in the garden of the palatial **El Asador d'Aranda** (see p123).

AFTERNOON

After you've had your fill of fine Castilian cuisine, stroll up Av Tibidabo to Plaça Doctor Andreu, where you can hop on the funicular train to go higher still to Plaça de Tibidabo. Pop into the **Parc d'Atraccions** (see p117) for a ride on the dodgems or the Ferris wheel. Then head to the landmark **Torre de Collserola** (see p117), where a glass elevator whisks you up to an observation deck for spectacular views. Return to Pl Doctor Andreu on the funicular and treat yourself to a *granissat* (see p65) in one of the terrace bars. Then ride down Av Tibidabo on the charming **Tramvia Blau** and catch the Bus Turístic back to the city centre.

See map on pp116–17

Gràcia Boutiques

Contemporary fashion at Boo

1 Boo
C/Bonavista 2

This elegantly decorated space offers contemporary clothing and accessories with a slightly vintage feel for men and women. Shoppers will find international labels like Saint James, Norse Projects and beautifully tailored shirts by Tuk Tuk. There's also a small selection of books and perfumes.

2 Lydia Delgado
C/Séneca 28

This well-established Catalan designer creates superbly cut clothing for women inspired by the 1950s and 1960s. Touches of embroidery, patchwork and other artistic details enliven the fabrics.

3 José Rivero
C/Astúries 43

José provides his own original in-house creations for men and women; he also sells accessories, including handbags, crafted by young local designers.

4 Berta Sumpsi
MAP F1 ▪ C/Verdi 98

This little space doubles as a workshop and showroom. There is an unusual range of simple and sculptural jewellery displayed in beautiful, minimal surroundings.

5 Érase Una Vez
C/Goya 7

The name of the store means "once upon a time", and indeed many a storybook fantasy comes true at this lovely shop, which creates fabulous, one-of-a-kind wedding gowns. It also stocks some of the most exclusive designers.

6 Món de Mones
C/Xiquets de Valls 9

For a range of striking jewellery and accessories, visit this charming little shop near the Plaça del Sol. Designer Teresa Roig uses a variety of materials, from glass to felt, to create her original designs.

7 Rock 01 Baby
C/Bonavista 16

Dress your baby in the latest fashions from this little shop, which has funky slogan T-shirts, Babygros and mini Ugg boots for the pint-sized hipster.

8 Mushi Mushi
C/Bonavista 12

From hard-to-find small labels to the best international collections, Mushi Mushi stocks a fine selection of women's fashion. There is also a small range of bags, shoes and other accessories.

9 El Piano
C/Verdi 20 bis

El Piano sells elegant and stylish womenswear with a retro flair made by Catalan designer Tina García. It also stocks clothes by other independent designers.

10 Botó and Co
C/Bonavista 3

This is the third and newest of the Botó and Co boutiques in Barcelona, selling high-quality fashion for women, including Current/Elliot jeans, Humanoid sweaters, and Sigerson Morrison footwear.

Gràcia Cafés

 Cafè del Sol
Pl del Sol 16

This café-bar is a cut above the others in the lively, bohemian Plaça del Sol. The atmosphere buzzes, the conversation inspires and the excellent coffee keeps on coming.

2 Cafè Salambó
C/Torrijos 51

Scrumptious sandwiches and a tasty range of salads are the draw at this beautiful bar-cum-café. There are pool tables upstairs.

3 Bar Quimet
MAP E1 ■ C/Vic 23

An authentic, old-fashioned bar with marble-topped tables and big wooden barrels, this is a great spot for an aperitif. Try the *vermut* (vermouth) and a selection of olives and *boquerones* (fresh anchovies).

 La Cafetera
Pl de la Virreina 2

Of all the cafés on Plaça de la Virreina, this one, with its outdoor terrace and tiny patio full of potted plants, is perhaps the nicest for a quiet and leisurely morning coffee and a sandwich or pastry.

5 Suís
Travessera de Gràcia 151

A colourful café that sells great ice creams and fresh fruit juices in summer, plus hot chocolate (which, with added whipped cream, is known as a *suís*) and a wide range of teas in winter. There are cakes and brownies too.

 Mama's Café
MAP F1 ■ C/Torrijos 26
■ Closed Tue

A pretty minimalist café with a small patio at the back. Organic sandwiches, salads and home-made cakes are served all day, as well as fresh fruit juices and cocktails.

 Onna Coffee
MAP E1 ■ C/Santa Teresa 1

This tiny coffee bar attracts the hipster set of Gràcia with its house-roasted coffee beans. You will also find a range of tasty home-made cakes and healthy sandwiches to choose from.

8 Cafè del Teatre
C/Torrijos 41

This is a great place to find a young, friendly crowd and good conversation. The only connection with the theatre, however, seems to be the velvet curtains on the sign over the door of this scruffy yet popular café.

 La Nena
MAP F1 ■ C/Ramón y Cajal 36

This café is popular with parents of young children, thanks to the room with tables and games for children. Their range of homemade cakes, juices and hot drinks make this a neighbourhood favourite.

10 Le Standard
C/Topazi 24 ■ Open
6pm–2:30am Tue–Sun

Like a granny's retro living room with leather sofas and floral wallpaper, Le Standard is the perfect spot to relax and enjoy a drink. They also organize cultural activities and exhibitions. Free Wi-Fi.

Retro interior of Le Standard

See map on pp116–17

Hip Drinking Spots

The bar area at Bobby Gin

1 Bobby Gin
MAP E1 ■ C/Francisco Giner 47

This cocktail bar stocks some 60 premium gins – floral, citric, spiced and vintage. Their slogan, "Respect the gin", comes courtesy of the eponymous bartender.

2 Universal
C/Marià Cubí 182 ■ Closed Sun ■ Occasional adm

Open until 5:30am, Universal is a two-level bar with a spacious, airy interior. The image-conscious crowd goes to flirt and dance to house (upstairs) and acid jazz.

3 Mirablau
Pl Dr Andreu ■ Open from 11am daily

A slightly older, well-heeled set who adhere to the smart dress code come to this club-bar for a combination of cocktails and amazing views of the city.

4 Gimlet
C/Santaló 46 ■ Open from 6pm Mon–Sat

Opened in 1982 by Javier de las Muelas, a well-known name on the international cocktail scene, Gimlet is a classic bar with contemporary flair, where you can enjoy premium drinks in elegant surroundings.

5 Luz de Gas
MAP D1 ■ C/Muntaner 246 ■ Open Wed–Sat

A major player since the mid-1990s, this club has occasional live Latin music until around midnight. After that it turns into a popular disco, attracting a slightly older crowd.

6 Velcro Bar
MAP F1 ■ C/Vallfogona 10

A tiny bar with a retro-style elegant interior, serving some excellent cocktails. It's a great place to start a night out, as it can get crowded in the later hours.

7 Otto Zutz
C/Lincoln 15 ■ Closed Sun ■ Adm

Barcelona's media crowd flock to this New-York-style club to chatter in the corners upstairs and shoot pool downstairs. The huge dance floors throb with house music *(see p58)*.

8 La Cervesera Artesana
MAP F1 ■ C/Sant Agustí 14 ■ Open from 6pm daily

This friendly microbrewery serves a good range of imported beers in addition to their own excellent brews. The Iberian Pale Ale, a mellow amber beer, is well worth a try.

9 Ajoblanco
MAP E1 ■ C/ Tuset 20 ■ Open from 8am daily

Mediterranean dishes and tapas are served here in the evening; then, at around midnight, a DJ sets up in the bar and a fashionable crowd rolls in to dance to classic tunes and enjoy gigantic gin and tonics.

10 Bikini
Av Diagonal 547 ■ Closed Sun–Wed ■ Adm

Open from midnight, this huge venue has three spaces, offering dance and Latin music and a cocktail lounge. Regular live music includes some of the best acts in Europe.

Restaurants and Tapas Bars

1 **El Asador d'Aranda**
Av Tibidabo 31 ■ 93 417 01 15
■ Closed Sun dinner (except Jun–Oct)
■ €€

Set in the magnificent *Modernista* Casa Roviralta, this restaurant is a magnet for businesspeople. Order the delicious lamb roasted in an oak-burning oven and dine in the beautiful garden *(see p62)*.

2 **Hofmann**
C/La Granada del Penedès 14–16 ■ 93 218 71 65 ■ Closed Sat lunch, Sun, Easter Week, Aug, Christmas ■ €€€

Run by talented chef Mey Hofmann, this Michelin-starred place serves exceptional Catalan cuisine. Save room for the exceptional desserts.

3 **Abissínia**
C/Torrent de les Flors 55
■ 93 213 07 85 ■ Closed Tue ■ €

Traditional Ethiopian stews are served with *injera* bread at this restaurant. Good for vegetarians.

4 **Il Giardinetto**
MAP E1 ■ C/La Granada del Penedès 28 ■ 93 218 75 36
■ Closed Sat lunch, Sun ■ €€

This eatery features whimsical, garden-themed decor and serves classic Mediterranean dishes such as spaghetti alla Sofia Loren (pasta with anchovy and parsley sauce).

5 **Fragments Café**
Pl de la Concòrdia 12
■ 93 419 96 13 ■ Closed Mon ■ €

Plaça de la Concòrdia, in the Les Corts neighbourhood, retains a small-town appeal. This sweet little café serves gourmet tapas out on the terrace or in its cosy interior.

6 **Bonanova**
C/Sant Gervasi de Cassoles 103
■ 93 417 10 33 ■ Closed Sun dinner, Mon ■ €€

Away from the tourist routes, Bonanova has been serving fresh, seasonal fare cooked in a simple and traditional way since 1964.

7 **La Balsa**
C/Infanta Isabel 4 ■ 93 211 50 48 ■ Closed Sun dinner, Mon, Easter, lunch in Aug ■ €€

With two garden terraces, La Balsa is a beautiful spot in the quiet Bonanova area, serving fine Basque, Catalan and Mediterranean dishes.

8 **El Vell Sarrià**
C/Major de Sarrià 93 ■ 93 204 57 10 ■ Closed Sun dinner, Mon ■ €€

Housed in a handsome old town house, this is the best place in the area for paellas, local rice dishes and grilled seafood.

9 **Botafumeiro**
C/Gran de Gràcia 81 ■ 93 218 42 30 (book ahead) ■ DA ■ €€€

The fish tanks at this seafood place teem with crabs and lobsters destined for dinner plates. Try the *pulpo Gallego* (Galician octopus).

10 **Acontraluz**
C/Milanesat 19 ■ 93 203 06 58
■ €€

This restaurant in a quiet part of town has a charming terrace and a retractable roof for alfresco dining. The modern Catalan menu includes a range of tapas.

Acontraluz restaurant

See map on pp116–17

🔟 Beyond Barcelona

Steeped in tradition, with its own language and pride in its identity, Catalonia is rich in both cultural heritage and physical beauty. It is not hyperbole to say that Catalonia has everything. The coastline has beautiful sandy beaches, intimate rocky coves and clear waters, while to the north are the 3,000-m (9,840-ft) Pyrenean peaks. These natural treasures are complemented by fabulous churches and monasteries in stunning mountain settings. The cuisine is rewarding, while the local *cava* holds its own against its French champagne counterparts.

Teatre-Museu Dalí

BEYOND BARCELONA

1 Montserrat

Tourist Information: Pl de la Creu ■ 93 877 77 01 ■ www.montserratvisita.com

The dramatic Montserrat mountain, with its remote Benedictine monastery (dating from 1025), is a religious symbol and a place of pilgrimage for the Catalan people. The basilica houses a statue of the patron saint of Catalonia, La Moreneta, also known as the "Black Virgin" *(see p41)*. Some legends date the statue to AD 50, but research suggests it was carved in the 12th century. The monastery was largely destroyed in 1811, during the War of Independence, and rebuilt some 30 years later.

The monastery at Montserrat

Montserrat – Catalan for "jagged mountain" – forms part of a ridge that rises suddenly from the plains. Take the funicular up to the peaks, where paths run alongside spectacular gorges to numerous hermitages.

2 Teatre-Museu Dalí, Figueres

Pl Gala-Salvador Dalí, Figueres ■ 97 267 75 00 ■ Open Mar–Jun & Oct: 9:30am–6pm Tue–Sun (Jun: daily); Jul–Sep: 9am–8pm daily (Aug: also 10pm–12:30am); Nov–Feb: 10:30am–6pm Tue–Sun ■ Adm ■ Casa-Museu Salvador Dalí: Portlligat, Cadaqués ■ 97 225 10 15 ■ Open Tue–Sun (mid-Jun to mid-Sep: daily) for guided visits only, by reservation; closed mid-Jan to mid-Feb ■ Adm ■ www.salvador-dali.org

Salvador Dalí was born in the town of Figueres in 1904. Paying tribute to the artist is the fantastic Teatre-Museu Dalí, which is full of his eccentric works. Housed in a former theatre, the country's second-most-visited museum (after the Prado in Madrid) provides a unique insight into the artist's extraordinary creations, from *La Cesta de Pan* (1926) to *El Torero Alucinógeno* (1970). A 30-minute drive away, near the beach town of Cadaqués, the Dalí connection continues. Here, you can visit the Casa-Museu Salvador Dalí, which served as the artist's summer home for nearly 60 years until his death in 1989.

	Top 10 Sights *see pp124–7*
	Places to Eat *see p131*
	Outdoor Activities *see p130*
	National Parks and Nature Reserves *see p129*
	Churches and Monasteries *see p128*

3 Costa Brava

The Costa Brava is a beautiful stretch of Mediterranean coastline, which runs from Blanes (about 60 km/37 miles north of Barcelona) all the way to the French border. There are a few big resorts, including Lloret de Mar and Roses, but many of the towns and resorts here, such as Calella de Palfrugell and Tamariu, have remained refreshingly low-key. Cultural highlights include the medieval citadel that crowns Tossa de Mar, and the Thyssen Museum in Sant Feliu de Guíxols. The area also has some excellent seafront hiking paths, the Camins de Ronda.

4 Alt Penedès

Tourist Information:
C/Hermengild Ciascar 2, Vilafranca del Penedès ▪ 93 818 12 54 ▪ Contact the tourist office for details on all winery visits in the region ▪ www. turismevilafranca.com

Catalonia's most famous wine region is the *cava*-producing area of the Penedès. The *cava* brands of Cordoníu and Freixenet have become household names worldwide. Many of the area's wineries and bodegas are open to the public. Cordoníu's is one of the most spectacular, housed in a *Modernista* building designed by Puig i Cadafalch, with a phenomenal 26 km (16 miles) of cellars on five floors.

5 Begur and around

Tourist Information:
Av Onze de Setembre 5 ▪ 97 262 45 20 ▪ www.begur.cat

The elegant hilltop town of Begur, with its ruined 14th-century castle, looks down over pristine wetlands and some of the prettiest coves on the Costa Brava. The town's population quadruples in summer as visitors make this their base for exploring nearby beaches and small, isolated coves. Many of the area's beaches stage jazz concerts during the summer. This is perhaps the best stretch of coastline in Catalonia.

Ruins of Tarragona's Roman wall

6 Tarragona

Tourist Information: C/Major 39 ▪ 97 725 07 95 ▪ www.tarragona turisme.cat

Now a huge industrial port, Tarragona was once the capital of Roman Catalonia, and the city's main attractions are from this era. Archaeological treasures include an impressive amphitheatre and the well-preserved Roman walls that lead past the Museu Nacional Arqueològic and the Torre de Pilatos, where Christians were supposedly imprisoned before being thrown to the lions. The Catedral de Santa Tecla is also in Tarragona *(see p128)*.

7 Girona

Tourist Information: Rambla de la Llibertat 1 ▪ 972 01 00 01 ▪ www.girona.cat/turisme

Girona is a beautiful town surrounded by lush green hills. Hidden away in the old town, the atmospheric Jewish quarter, known as El Call, is one of Europe's best-preserved medieval enclaves. Visiting Girona's cathedral is a must *(see p128)*.

Statue, El Call

(8) Empúries

C/Puig i Cadafalch s/n, Empúries ■ 97 277 02 08 ■ Open 10am–5pm (June–Sep: to 8pm, Oct–mid-Nov & mid-Feb–May: to 6pm) ■ Adm; free last Tue of month Oct–Jun

After Tarragona, Empúries is Catalonia's second most important Roman site. Occupying an impressive position by the sea, it comprises more than 40 ha (99 acres) scattered with Greek and Roman ruins, the highlights of which are the remains of a market street, various temples and a Roman amphitheatre. It's an ideal spot for those looking to mix a bit of history with a dip in the sea.

(9) Port Aventura

Av Pere Molas, Vila-seca, Tarragona ■ 90 220 22 20 ■ For opening times see website ■ Adm ■ www.portaventuraworld.com

This theme park is divided into six areas, including the Far West and Polynesia, and has some of Europe's biggest rollercoasters, as well as a thrilling Ferrari Land.

(10) Costa Daurada and Sitges

Tourist Information: Pl Eduard Maristany 2, Sitges ■ 93 894 42 51 ■ www.sitgestur.cat

With its wide sandy beaches and shallow waters, the Costa Daurada differs from the northern Catalonian coastline. Sleepy Torredembarra is a pleasant family resort, but the jewel in the crown is Sitges, the summer home to Barcelona's chic crowd, and a popular gay destination (see p61). Despite its frenetic feel, Sitges never reaches the tacky excesses of some of the Costa Brava's towns.

Sitges

A SCENIC DRIVE

↑ From Barcelona (85km)

▶ **MORNING**

This drive should take about 5 hours for the round trip. From Barcelona take the AP7 motorway until exit 4, then take the C260 to Cadaqués. Just before dropping down to the town, stop at the viewpoint and take in the azure coastline and the whitewashed houses of this former fishing village. Once in **Cadaqués**, now one of Catalonia's trendiest beach towns, wander the charming boutique-filled streets. After a splash in the sea and a coffee at one of the chic terrace cafés, take the road leaving Port Lligat and head for the **Cap de Creus** (see p129) lighthouse. Drive through the desolately beautiful landscape of this rocky headland before doubling back and heading off to **Port de la Selva**. The road twists and winds interminably, but the picture-perfect scenery will leave you speechless.

AFTERNOON

Enjoy a seafood lunch at Ca l'Herminda (C/Illa 7), in the small, mountain-enclosed Port de la Selva. Then drive to the neighbouring village of **Selva del Mar**, with its tiny river, for a post-prandial coffee on the terrace of the Bar Stop (C/Port de la Selva 1), before continuing up to the **Monestir de Sant Pere de Rodes** (see p128). You'll be tempted to stop frequently on the way up to take in the views. Don't, because the best is to be had from the monastery itself – a sweeping vista of the whole area. There are plenty of well-signposted walks around the mountain top, and it is worth sticking around to see the sun set slowly over the bay.

See map on pp124–5 ←

Churches and Monasteries

1 Monestir de Montserrat
Montserrat ■ 93 877 77 01
■ Adm to museums, basilica free
■ www.abadiamontserrat.cat
Catalonia's holiest place and its most visited monastery boasts beautiful Romanesque art and a statue of the "Black Virgin" (see p125).

2 Monestir de Poblet
Off N240, 10 km W of Montblanc ■ Adm ■ www.poblet.cat
This busy working monastery contains the Gothic Capella de Sant Jordi, a Romanesque church, and the Porta Daurada, a doorway that was gilded for Felipe II's visit in 1564.

3 Monestir de Ripoll
Ripoll ■ 97 270 42 03
■ www.monestirderipoll.cat ■ Adm
The west portal of this monastery (879) has reputedly the finest Romanesque carvings in Spain. Of the original buildings, only the doorway and cloister remain.

4 Monestir de Santes Creus
Santes Creus, 25 km NW of Montblanc ■ 97 763 83 29 ■ Closed Mon ■ Adm ■ www.mhcat.cat
The cloister at this Gothic treasure (1150) is notable for the beautifully sculpted panels by English artist Reinard Funoll.

5 Sant Joan de les Abadesses
Sant Joan de les Abadesses ■ 97 272 05 99 ■ www.santjoandeles abadesses.com ■ Adm
This monastery, established in the 9th century, boasts a magnificent Romanesque sculpture representing the Descent from the Cross.

6 Sant Climent i Santa Maria de Taüll
138 km N of Lleida ■ 97 369 67 15
■ www.centreromanic.com
These two Romanesque churches, dating from 1123, are perfect examples of those that pepper the Pyrenees. The frescoes are reproductions of the originals, now in Barcelona's MNAC (see pp20–21).

7 Catedral de La Seu d'Urgell
La Seu d'Urgell ■ 97 335 32 42
■ Adm
Dating from around 1040, this cathedral is one of the most elegant in Catalonia.

8 Catedral de Girona
Plaça de la Catedral s/n, Girona ■ 97 242 71 89 ■ Adm; Mass & Sun free ■ www.catedraldegirona.cat
This cathedral possesses the widest Gothic nave in Europe and the second widest after the basilica in the Vatican.

9 Catedral de Santa Tecla
Old Town, Tarragona
■ Closed Sun ■ Adm ■ Guided tours
■ www.catedraldetarragona.com
At 104 m (340 ft) long, Tarragona's cathedral is the largest in the region. Its architecture is a mixture of Gothic and Romanesque.

10 Monestir de Sant Pere de Rodes
22 km E of Figueres ■ Closed Mon
■ Adm ■ www.mhcat.cat
The dilapidated charm of this UNESCO World Heritage Site may have dwindled since its face-lift, but its views over Cap de Creus and Port de la Selva are still breathtaking.

Monestir de Sant Pere de Rodes

National Parks and Nature Reserves

 Parc Nacional d'Aigüestortes i Estany de Sant Maurici

148 km N of Lleida

The magnificent peaks of Catalonia's only national park are accessible from the village of Espot. You'll find waterfalls, lakes and glacial tarns 2,000 m (6,560 ft) up.

 Delta de l'Ebre

28 km SE of Tortosa

This giant delta is a patchwork of paddy fields. The wide expanse of the River Ebre is a nature reserve for migratory birds and has scores of bird-watching stations.

 Parc Natural de la Zona Volcànica de la Garrotxa

40 km NW of Girona

La Garrotxa last erupted 10,000 years ago and the zone's other volcanoes are long since extinct. The largest crater is the Santa Margalida, at 500 m (1,640 ft) wide. It is best to visit in spring, when thousands of butterflies emerge.

Purple heron, Delta de l'Ebre

④ **Cap de Creus**

36 km E of Figueres

As the Pyrenees tumble into the Mediterranean, they create a rocky headland, jutting out 10 km (6.25 miles). This forms Catalonia's most easterly point and offers spectacular views of the craggy coastline.

⑤ **Parc Natural del Cadí-Moixeró**

20 km E of La Seu d'Urgell

Covered in a carpet of conifers and oaks, this mountain range is overgrown with lush vegetation. Several of the peaks here are over 2,000 m (6,560 ft) high.

⑥ **Parc Natural del Montseny**

48 km NW of Barcelona

Forming Catalonia's most accessible natural park, these woodland hills are well-equipped for walkers and mountain bikers, with a vast network of trails. Take the popular and well-signposted climb up Turó de l'Home, which is the highest peak.

⑦ **Massís de Pedraforca**

64 km N of Manresa

A nature reserve surrounds this huge outcrop of mountains, a favourite of rock climbers with peaks rising to 2,500 m (8,200 ft).

⑧ **Serra de l'Albera**

15 km N of Figueres

On the eastern part of the border between Spain and France, the tree-covered slopes of the Albera Massif are dotted with about 20 Romanesque churches in different states of preservation.

⑨ **Parc Natural dels Aiguamolls de l'Empordà**

15 km E of Figueres

This nature reserve hides a number of birdwatching towers. Those in the Laguna de Vilalt and La Bassa de Gall Mari allow the observation of herons, moorhens and other bird species nesting in spring.

⑩ **Parc Natural de Sant Llorenç del Munt**

12 km E of Manresa

Surrounded by industry and within easy reach of Barcelona, this untamed park is inhabited by large numbers of wild boar. Walk up Cerro de la Mola to see the Romanesque monastery, which is now a restaurant.

See map on pp124–5

Outdoor Activities

Rafting on La Noguera Pallaresa

1 Rafting and Kayaking
Noguera Aventura, Lleida ▪ 97 329 01 76 ▪ www.noguera ventura.com

One of Europe's best rivers for whitewater sports is La Noguera Pallaresa in the Pyrenees. Late spring is the best time to go, as the mountain snow begins to thaw.

2 Scuba Diving
Aquàtica, L'Estartit ▪ 97 275 06 56 ▪ www.aquatica-sub.com

The Reserva Natural de les Illes Medes has thousands of species of fish and red coral reefs. Glass-bottom boats cater to non-divers.

3 Water Sports and Sailing
Club de Mar Sitges, Pg Marítim, Sitges ▪ 93 894 09 05 ▪ www.club marsitges.com

Good sailing can be found in Sitges, along with yachts for rent and classes for novices. Canoeing and windsurfing are also available.

4 Skiing
La Molina: 25 km S of Puigcerdà ▪ 97 289 20 31 ▪ www.lamolina.cat ▪ Baqueira-Beret: 14 km E of Vielha ▪ 90 241 54 15 ▪ www.baqueira.es

La Molina is the most accessible Pyrenean ski-resort from Barcelona, but Baqueira-Beret is where the jet-set goes. Both offer all levels of skiing (including off-piste) from December onwards.

5 Golf
Santa Cristina d'Aro: 97 283 70 55 ▪ Platja d'Aro: 97 281 67 27

The Costa Brava is one of Europe's top golf destinations; the best courses are around Platja d'Aro.

6 Horse Riding
Hípica Can Tramp, Ctra Cànoves ▪ 93 871 16 08 ▪ www. hipicacantramp.es

Montseny Natural Park *(see p129)* is ideal for horse riding, with a number of stables.

7 Ballooning
Vol de Coloms ▪ 97 268 02 55 or 68 9471 872 ▪ www.voldecoloms.cat

A balloon journey over the volcanic area of La Garrotxa is an unbeatable way to get a bird's-eye view of the beautiful Catalonian landscape.

8 Boat Trips
Dofi Jet Boats, Blanes ▪ 97 235 20 21 ▪ Boats every hour daily from Blanes and Lloret de Mar (twice daily from Calella); closed Nov–Mar ▪ www.dofijetboats.com

Take a cruise from Calella and Blanes along the Costa Brava, stopping at the old town and medieval castle of Tossa de Mar.

9 Activities at the Canal Olímpic
Canal Olímpic ▪ Av Canal Olímpic, Castelldefels ▪ 93 636 28 96 ▪ www.canalolimpic.cat

Used for rowing competitions in the 1992 Olympics, the huge Canal Olímpic is now a leisure complex offering a host of activities.

10 Foraging for Mushrooms
From late September to late October, thousands of Catalans flock to the hills in search of the highly-prized *rovelló* mushrooms. Some varieties are poisonous, so amateurs should first make sure they get a reliable guide through the Diputació de Barcelona (www.diba.cat).

Places to Eat

PRICE CATEGORIES

For a three-course meal for one with half a bottle of wine (or equivalent meal), including taxes and extra charges.

€ under €35 €€ €35–50 €€€ over €50

1 Tragamar
Platja de Canadell s/n, Callella de Palafrugell ■ 97 261 43 36 ■ €€
Book ahead for a table on the terrace or by one of the bay windows at this beachside restaurant, and enjoy stellar seafood dishes such as tuna carpaccio or lobster paella.

2 Les Cols
Mas les Cols, Ctra de la Canya s/n, Olot ■ 97 226 92 09 ■ www.lescols.com ■ Closed Sun & Tue eves, Mon ■ €€€
Two-Michelin-starred Les Cols prepares contemporary Spanish cuisine with home-grown vegetables and local seasonal produce in a stunning modern setting.

3 La Torre del Remei
Camí del Remei 3, Bolvir, Cerdanya, 3 km SW of Puigcerdà ■ 97 214 01 82 ■ €€
A *Modernista* palace provides an elegant setting for wonderfully presented Catalan food.

4 Cal Ticus
C/Raval 19, Sant Sadurní d'Anoia ■ 93 818 41 60 ■ Closed Sun–Wed eves ■ €
This modern restaurant serves traditional cuisine using seasonal products from nearby suppliers. A good selection of Penedès wines are on the list and for sale in their shop.

5 Fonda Europa
C/Anselm Clavé 1, Granollers ■ 93 870 03 12 ■ €€
Established in 1771, Fonda Europa was the first in a line of successful Catalan restaurants. Dishes include pig's trotters and a Catalan stockpot with meat and vegetables.

6 Lasal de Varador
Pg Marítim 1, Mataró ■ 93 114 05 80 ■ Closed mid-Oct–May: eves daily, Mon & Tue ■ €€
This beachfront restaurant serves tasty paellas, seafood and a range of other dishes, using organic and sustainably sourced ingredients.

7 Sant Pau
C/Nou 10, Sant Pol de Mar ■ 93 760 06 62 ■ Closed Sun, Mon, Thu lunch, 3 weeks May, 3 weeks Nov ■ €€€
Carme Ruscalleda is said to be one of the finest chefs in the country. Her three-Michelin-starred restaurant offers sublime Catalan cuisine.

8 Can Roura
C/Major 10, Sant Martí d'Empúries, l'Escala ■ 97 277 33 80 ■ Closed mid-Sep–May; call for opening times ■ €
Opened in 1958 and now run by the founder's grandson. Sample some of the best traditional cuisine in the area, including the freshest local fish.

9 El Celler de Can Roca
C/Can Sunyer 48, Girona ■ 97 222 21 57 ■ Book online well in advance ■ www.cellercanroca.com ■ €€€
The Roca brothers' exciting Catalan cuisine is complemented by great wines. The restaurant has three Michelin stars and an 11-month waiting list.

Dessert, El Celler de Can Roca

10 Cal Ton
C/Casal 8, Vilafranca del Penedès ■ 93 890 37 41 ■ Closed Mon, Sun eve, Easter, 3 weeks Aug ■ €€
Contemporary cuisine in the heart of Catalonia's biggest wine region. Order the *menu degustació*.

See map on pp124–5

Streetsmart

**Looking down on the two entrance
pavilions at Park Güell**

Getting To and Around Barcelona

Arriving by Air

Most flights arrive at **El Prat Airport**, located 12 km (7.5 miles) south of the city centre. The airport has two terminals, linked by a shuttle bus. Local train services run every 30 minutes to the city centre, (about 25 mins), while metro Line 9 Sud links Zona Universitària station (Line 3) on the western side of the city (about 30 mins). There is also an express airport bus service, **Aerobús** (20–30 mins).

There are taxi ranks at both terminals (€25–35 into central Barcelona), as well as several car rental companies.

Iberia offers a shuttle service between Madrid and Barcelona with up to 30 flights a day, and also links to many other domestic destinations, as do **Vueling** and **Air Europa**. There are direct flights on national and low-cost airlines from the UK and most major European cities. Some low-cost and charter airlines also fly to Girona and Reus, both about 100 km (62 miles) away. There are direct flights from New York, Miami and Atlanta, and flights from Australia and New Zealand via Dubai and other stopovers.

Arriving by Train

Services are operated by Spain's national rail company, **RENFE**, and by the Catalan government's **FGC** (Ferrocarrils de la Generalitat de Catalunya).

Inter-city and European trains use Estació de Sants and Estació de França (a new high-speed train station, Sagrera, is under construction). Sants offers a number of facilities, including lockers, ATMs and bureaux de change, but França has none. The fast AVE train from Sants connects Barcelona to Madrid in under 3 hours.

Arriving by Road

Several bus companies link Barcelona to Spain's major cities, and both **Eurolines** and **Alsa** connect from major European cities. Book tickets online through **Movelia**. Most buses operate from **Estació del Nord** (timetables are available on its website) and from a smaller station next to Estació de Sants.

Those arriving by car will find good autopistes (tolled highways) and toll-free roads linking Europe and the rest of Spain to Barcelona. The tolled AP7 runs from the French border to Barcelona.

Travelling by Metro and Train

Transports Metropolitans de Barcelona or **TMB** operates the extensive public transport network in the city and suburbs, covering the funicular, bus, metro, RENFE and FGC. The eight-line metro system (L1–L5, L9–L11) is fast, convenient and easy to use. It runs from 5am to midnight Monday to Thursday, 5am to 2am

Friday, and 5am Saturday to midnight on Sunday. TMB's website has travel information, route finders and schedules.

Barcelona has two local train operators: RENFE runs rodalies (cercanías in Spanish) to towns around the city and the airport; FGC runs the commuter rail system (L6, L7, L8) in eastern and northern Barcelona. Both RENFE and FGC share some key stations with the metro.

By Bus and Tram

Barcelona's bus system covers the entire city. Bus stops are clearly marked and buses display their destinations on the front. Most routes run from 4:30am to 11pm daily. Nitbús (night bus) routes, operated by **ATM**, usually run from 10:40pm to 6am. For schedules and routes, check the ATM website or pick up a bus guide from the tourist office.

Barcelona has two tram lines, Trambaix (T1, T2, T3) and Trambesòs (T4, T5, T6), which run between 4:55am and 12:30am daily (each line has slightly different hours). They are operated by **TRAM**, whose website has route and schedule information.

TMB operates Tramvia Blau, a heritage tram line linking L7 with the funicular (buy tickets from the conductor; cash only).

Tickets

The city's integrated fare system covers bus, tram,

metro, local train and *rodalies*. A single fare costs €2.15. The T-10 multiperson travel card is valid for 10 trips in zones 1 to 6 (the total journey must be completed within 75 minutes. The T-Dia card offers unlimited daily travel for an individual. Tickets can be bought from machines at metro stations. The Hola BCN! pass can be bought via the TMB website or from machines at stations for 2, 3, 4 or 5 days of unlimited travel on public transport, including the airport metro line.

By Taxi

You can hail a yellow-and-black taxi in the street; a green light on the roof indicates it is free. Taxis can be ordered online or on the phone from **Taxi Ecològic**, **Radio Taxi 033**, **Barna Taxi**, **Taxi Class** and **Taxi Amic** (adapted for disabled travellers). For two or more passengers, taxis are almost as cheap as the metro for short hops. There is a minimum fare, and supplements for luggage, for port and airport trips, journeys at night and on public holidays, and from the rank at Sants station.

By Car

Driving in the city is not recommended. The narrow roads and one-way systems are tricky to negotiate and street parking is difficult to find. Those arriving by car are advised to leave it in a covered car park on the outskirts and use public transport.

By Bicycle

Cycling can be a fun alternative to walking. Barcelona has more than 180 km (112 miles) of bike lanes: maps are available from the tourist office and rental shops, such as **Budget Bikes**, **Rabbit Bike** and **Bikeceloning** *(see p140)*. The city's **Bicing** scheme, which allows people to pick up and drop off bikes from stands across town, is geared towards residents – there's an annual charge and you need a local address. You can also get around by scooter, motorbike or Segway. Ask the tourist office for a list of local rental companies.

On Foot

Most areas are best seen on foot, especially the old town and Gràcia, where a leisurely stroll is the only way to soak up the architectural and cultural riches. The seafront, from Port Vell to Port Olímpic, is also great for walking.

DIRECTORY

ARRIVING BY AIR

Aerobús
w aerobusbcn.com

Air Europa
w aireuropa.com

El Prat Airport
w aena.es

Iberia
w iberia.com

Vueling
w vueling.com

ARRIVING BY TRAIN

FGC
w fgc.cat

RENFE
w renfe.com

ARRIVING BY ROAD

Alsa
w alsa.com

Estació del Nord
C/Ali Bei 80
w barcelonanord.cat

Eurolines
w eurolines.es

Movelia
w movelia.com

METRO AND TRAIN

TMB
w tmb.cat

BUS AND TRAM

ATM
w atm.cat

TRAM
w tram.cat

TAXI COMPANIES

Barna Taxi
w barnataxi.com

Radio Taxi 033
w radiotaxi033.com

Taxi Amic
w taxi-amic-adaptat.com

Taxi Class
w taxiclassrent.com

Taxi Ecològic
w taxiecologic.com

BICYCLE HIRE

Bikeceloning
w bikeceloning.com

Bicing
w bicing.cat

Budget Bikes
w budgetbikes.eu

Rabbit Bike
w rabbitbike.es

Practical Information

Passports and Visas

Visitors from outside the European Economic Area (EEA), European Union (EU) and Switzerland need a valid passport to enter Spain. EEA, EU and Swiss nationals can use their national identity cards instead. Citizens of Canada, the US, Australia and New Zealand can visit Spain for up to 90 days without a visa as long as their passport is valid for 6 months beyond the date of entry. For longer stays, a visa is necessary and needs to be obtained in advance from the Spanish embassy. Most other non-EU nationals need a visa, and should consult the Citizen Services section of the Spanish **Ministry of Foreign Affairs and Cooperation** website or their Spanish embassy for details. Schengen visas are valid for Spain.

Customs and Immigration

For EU citizens there are no limits on most goods carried in or out of Spain, as long as they are only for personal use. Exceptions include firearms and weapons, some types of food and plants, and endangered species.

Passengers can import the following from EU countries: 800 cigarettes, 400 cigarillos, 200 cigars, 1 kg (2.2 lb) of smoking tobacco, 10 litres of spirits over 22 per cent proof, 20 litres of alcoholic beverages under 22 per cent, 90 litres of wine (no more than 60 litres of sparkling wine and 110 litres of beer. Passengers from non-EU countries can import 200 cigarettes or 250 g (9 oz) of tobacco products, and those above 20 may also bring 1 litre of spirits, 1 litre of wine and 6 litres of beer. Non-EU residents can claim back VAT on EU purchases over €90.15 at the airport when leaving the EU (see p140).

Travel Safety Advice

Visitors can get up-to-date travel safety information from the **Foreign and Commonwealth Office** in the UK, the **State Department** in the US and the **Department of Foreign Affairs and Trade** in Australia.

Travel Insurance

All travellers are advised to buy insurance against theft or loss, accidents, illness and travel delays or cancellations. Spain has a reciprocal health agreement with other EU countries, and EU citizens receive emergency treatment under the public healthcare system if they have a valid European Health Insurance Card (EHIC) with them. Dental care is not covered, and prescriptions may have to be paid for upfront. Non-EU visitors should check if their country has reciprocal arrangements with Spain.

Car hire agencies offer vehicle cover, but you might already be covered through your bank, travel or home policies.

Emergency Services

The ambulance, police and fire brigade can be reached on the Europe-wide emergency number **112**. There are also dedicated lines for the **Policía Nacional** (the national police force), the **Guàrdia Urbana** (the municipal police force), the **Mossos d'Esquadra** (the Catalonian police force) and **ambulance**.

Health

There are no vaccinations required for Spain, and there are few serious health hazards. Carry with you any prescriptions for medications that you take.

For minor ailments, go to a *farmàcia* (pharmacy). They are marked with a large red or green cross and are usually open from 10am to 9pm Monday to Saturday. When closed, they will post a sign giving the location of the nearest *farmàcia de guàrdia* which will be open. Pharmacies that are open 24 hours include the **Farmàcia Clapés** on La Rambla.

There are many clinics (usually private), including the **Creu Blanca Pelai**, where no appointment is needed. Major hospitals include **Hospital Dos de Maig** and **Hospital de la Santa Creu i de Sant Pau**.

Personal Security

Barcelona is a relatively safe city, although petty crimes such as pickpocketing and bag-snatching remain problematic. The usual advice to anyone travelling in a large city applies. Leave all your valuables, including your passport, in a hotel safety deposit box. Carry as little cash as possible and hide what you do have in a money belt under clothes. Carry wallets in front pockets and strap bags across your front. On the beach and in cafés and restaurants, keep your belongings on your lap or tied to your person. Be cautious of any odd or unnecessary human contact, verbal or physical, be it a tap on the shoulder or someone spilling their drink at your table. Thieves often work in pairs, and while one is distracting you, the other is swiping your wallet. Although serious incidences of violence are rare, thieves occasionally carry knives – hand over your belongings immediately if threatened. If you need to report a crime, go to the nearest *comissaria*. Although you may see police from other forces, contact is usually with the Mossos d'Esquadra, who wear navy blue uniforms.

Travellers with Specific Needs

Most modern restaurants, hotels, shops, malls and museums are accessible to wheelchair users, and the streets of Barcelona are constantly being improved. Many of the older buildings, however, remain inaccessible, so it is always worth calling in advance to find out what facilities are available.

All city buses and most metro and train stations are wheelchair accessible. Contact the **IMD** (Institut Municipal de Persones amb Discapacitat) information. **Disabled Accessible Travel** organizes tours and can give advice about city hotels. The **Viajes 2000** travel agency specializes in holidays for disabled travellers.

DIRECTORY

PASSPORTS AND VISAS

Ministry of Foreign Affairs and Cooperation
🌐 exteriores.gob.es

EMBASSIES AND CONSULATES

Australia
MAP D1 ▪ Av Diagonal 433 bis, Level 2, Door 1
🌐 spain.embassy.gov.au

Canada
MAP E3 ▪ Pl de Catalunya 9
🌐 canadainternational. gc.ca/spain-espagne/ offices-bureaux/ consul_barcelona.aspx

Ireland
Gran Via Carlos III 94
🌐 dfa.ie/irish-embassy/ spain

UK
MAP D1
▪ Av Diagonal 477
🌐 gov.uk/world/ organisations/ british-consulate-general-barcelona

USA
Paseo Reina Elisenda de Montcada 23
🌐 es.usembassy.gov

TRAVEL SAFETY ADVICE

Australia
Department of Foreign Affairs and Trade
🌐 dfat.gov.au
🌐 smartraveller.gov.au

UK
Foreign and Commonwealth Office
🌐 gov.uk/foreign-travel-advice

US
US Department of State
🌐 travel.state.gov

EMERGENCY SERVICES

Ambulance, Police and Fire Brigade
📞 112

Ambulance
📞 061

Guàrdia Urbana
📞 092

Mossos d'Esquadra
📞 112

Policía Nacional
📞 091

HEALTH

Creu Blanca Pelai
MAP L1 ▪ C/Pelayo 40
🌐 creu-blanca.es/en

Farmàcia Clapés
MAP L3 ▪ La Rambla 98
🌐 farmaciaclapes.com/ tienda

Hospital de la Santa Creu i de Sant Pau
MAP H1 ▪ C/Sant Antoni Maria Claret 167
🌐 santpau.cat

Hospital Dos de Maig
MAP H1 ▪ C/Dos de Maig 301
🌐 csi.cat

TRAVELLERS WITH SPECIFIC NEEDS

Disabled Accessible Travel
🌐 disabledaccessible travel.com

IMD
🌐 ajuntament. barcelona.cat/accessible

Viajes 2000
🌐 viajes2000.com

Currency and Banking

Spain uses the euro (€), which is divided into 100 cents. Paper notes are in denominations of €5, €10, €20, €50, €100, €200 and €500. Coins are €2, €1, 50c, 20c, 10c, 5c, 2c and 1c.

ATMs (cash machines) are the easiest way to get cash and are also a good way to beat commission charges. Surcharges depend on your bank.

Banks tend to offer better exchange and commission rates than bureaux de change, although rates do vary from bank to bank.

Pre-paid currency cards (cash passports) are a more secure way of carrying money. They can be preloaded with euros, fixing exchange rates before you leave, and used like a debit card.

Credit cards (apart from American Express) are widely accepted, except in small shops and restaurants, and there may be a minimum charge, generally €6–10. You will be asked for your card PIN number and/or photo ID. If your credit card is lost or stolen, inform the police and your credit card company.

Internet and Telephone

Many cafés, hotels and restaurants offer free Wi-Fi. Barcelona's city government also provides free Wi-Fi hotspots around the city.

The dialing code for Spain is 34 and Barcelona's city code is 93. Phone numbers must always be dialled in full, including the city code. Most mobile phones will work in Spain but it is advisable to check with your provider about costs. Consider buying a local SIM card or a pay-as-you-go mobile (both widely available) to avoid high roaming charges.

Postal Services

Main branches of Spain's **Correos** post offices are usually open 8:30am–8:30pm Monday to Friday and 9:30am–1pm on Saturdays. Suburban and village branches open 9am–2pm during the week and 9:30am–1pm Saturday. Mailboxes are painted bright yellow.

Television and Radio

Public national television includes the La Una and La Dos channels from Televisión Española, Catalonia's public station TV3, and the city's own Barcelona TV. There are also numerous private channels, and satellite television is widely available. Many television sets can be adjusted to broadcast shows in their original languages. Several regional stations broadcast mainly in Catalan, and there are six state Spanish radio stations.

Newspapers and Magazines

Newsstands along the Rambla have a variety of international publications. *La Vanguardia* and *El Periódico* (Catalan and Spanish editions) are the main local papers. *El País*, *ABC* and *El Mundo* are Spanish national dailies. The English-language online newspaper *The Local* has Spanish news, while the free *Barcelona Metropolitan* magazine (print and online) has listings plus articles on local topics. The free *Time Out Barcelona* magazine (print and online) is great for listings (Catalan only), as is the Catalan *Què Fem?* issued with Friday's *La Vanguardia*.

Opening Hours

Office hours are generally 9am–6pm Monday–Friday, although businesses do tend to shut at 2pm in August or close for the month. Shops are usually open 10am–2pm and 4–8pm. Larger shops and department stores don't close at lunchtime and are usually open until 9 or 10pm.

Banks generally open 8am–2pm on weekdays. Some banks also open 4–8pm on Thursdays and 8am–2pm on Saturdays, except July to September.

Museums and galleries have their own opening hours, which may change with the season. It is best to check their websites before you visit.

Most banks, stores and businesses are closed on public holidays: New Year's Day, Epiphany (6 Jan), Good Friday, Easter Sunday, Feast of Sant Jordi (23 Apr), Labour Day (1 May), Feast of Sant Joan (24 Jun), Ascension Day (15 Aug), Catalan Day (11 Sep), Hispanic Day (12 Oct), All Saints' Day (1 Nov), Constitution Day (6 Dec), Immaculate Conception (8 Dec),

Christmas Day (25 Dec), and the Feast of St Stephen (26 Dec).

Time Difference

Spain operates on Central European Time (CET), which is 1 hour ahead of Greenwich Mean Time (GMT) and 6 hours ahead of US Eastern Standard Time (EST). The clock moves forward 1 hour during daylight savings time, from the last Sunday in March until the last Sunday in November.

Electrical Appliances

Spain uses plugs with two round pins and an electrical voltage and frequency of 230V/50Hz. North American devices will need adaptors and voltage converters.

Driving Licences

All valid full European and US driving licences are accepted in Spain. It is recommended that non-EU visitors get an International Driving Permit (IDP), even though North Americans do not need one. To hire a car, you will also need a credit card and your passport.

Weather

The climate is typically Mediterranean, with cool winters and warm summers. July and August can be hot and humid, with temperatures reaching 35° C (95° F). January and February are the two coldest months, although temperatures rarely drop below 10° C (50° F).

Language

Catalan and Spanish are the official languages, and locals switch easily between the two. Though most will have at least a few words of English, they are delighted when tourists try to speak even a word or two in Catalan. Street names are posted exclusively in Catalan, while menus are printed in Spanish, Catalan and, less often, English.

Smoking

Smoking is completely prohibited in hotels, bars, restaurants, clubs, cafés and public transport. There are no designated smoking areas inside, and smoking outdoors is also restricted in certain areas.

Visitor Information

Multilingual staff give out free maps and information at the **Barcelona Turisme** main tourist information office at Plaça de Catalunya. They also have a useful accommodation booking service and bureau de change. There are additional Barcelona Turisme offices at the airport, La Rambla, Estació de Sants and Plaça de Sant Jaume, and booths at Estació del Nord, Plaça Espanya and other key tourist spots.

In summer red-jacketed tourist information officers roam the busiest areas giving out maps and advice. Barcelona Turisme's excellent website provides information, sells tickets and lets you book accommodation. It also has useful apps, including a general city

guide, as well as specific guides to Medieval Barcelona, Roman Barcelona and Gaudí's Barcelona.

The **Culture Institute** in the Palau de la Virreina offers information on cultural and arts events. The city council's website, **La Meva Barcelona**, and the **Turisme de Catalunya** office and website are also good sources of information.

Useful apps include Citymapper for transport information, TripAdvisor and Google Translate.

DIRECTORY

POSTAL SERVICES

Correos
🔳 correos.es

NEWSPAPERS AND MAGAZINES

Barcelona Metropolitan
🔳 barcelona-metropolitan.com

The Local
🔳 thelocal.es

Time Out Barcelona
🔳 timeout.cat

VISITOR INFORMATION

Barcelona Turisme
MAP M1 ◼ Pl de Catalunya 17
8:30am–9pm daily
📞 93 285 38 34
🔳 barcelonaturisme.com

Culture Institute
MAP L3 ◼ La Rambla 99
📞 93 316 10 00

La Meva Barcelona
🔳 lamevabarcelona.com

Turisme de Catalunya
MAP E2 ◼ Palau Robert, Pg de Gràcia 107
10am–8pm Mon–Sat (to 2:30pm Sun)
📞 93 238 80 91
🔳 catalunya.com

Trips and Tours

There are almost as many ways to visit Barcelona as there are visitors to the city. The **Bus Turístic** is the official, city-run hop-on hop-off bus tour. It runs three routes, which provide a convenient overview of the main sights. The red route explores northern Barcelona; the blue route takes in the southern area; and the green route travels along the seafront (April–September only). A night tour is also available.

If you prefer walking, try one of the excellent themed tours offered by the **Barcelona Turisme** office on Plaça Catalunya. Their website offers an overview of the available tours, plus a discount if you buy them online.

Fans of *Modernista* architecture can book onto Barcelona Turisme's *Modernista* walking tour, which visits the main sites in the Eixample area, or pick up the free **Ruta del Modernisme** map at the tourist office.

It's easy to hire bikes or scooters (see p135), and many bike rental places also conduct cycling tours of the city. **Bike Tours Barcelona** has several themed tours, including a *Modernista* cycling tour and a beach tour, while **Art Bike Tour** takes cyclists to the city's top contemporary galleries on two wheels. You can also explore the streets on a vintage-style Ural motorcycle and sidecar with **Bright Side Tours**.

If you're keen to try out something different, rent a Segway from **Barcelona Segway Tours** (tours start with a training session) or hire a **GoCar**, a cross between a two-person scooter and a small car. These tiny, open-top GPS-guided vehicles are ideal for pottering around the sights of Barcelona, and an audio tour is included in the price.

See the city from the air with a **Cat Helicopter** tour, or from the Mediterranean in the old-fashioned **Las Golondrinas** "swallow boats" or via an **Orsom Catamaran** tour.

Birding enthusiasts should check out **Catalan Bird Tours**, which organizes trips to the region's best bird-watching sites.

Shopping

Barcelona is a fantastic shopping destination, with all the major international stores and big Spanish brands represented, plus a great choice of small boutiques. Great buys include deli produce, such as hams, cheeses and olive oil, as well as superb Catalan wines. Check for any restrictions on importing foodstuffs into your home country before you buy. You'll also find unusual fashions, jewellery and objects for the home in the city's many one-off stores: the best areas to find these are El Born, which is full of stylish small boutiques, and Gràcia, where the shops have slightly edgier, more bohemian offerings.

There are also several outlet shops in the city, particularly on and around **Carrer Girona** (see p66). **La Roca Village**, an outlet shopping centre dedicated to designer brands, is located outside the city near Granollers.

There are two main sales periods, one beginning in early January and another starting on 1st July.

All prices include VAT (IVA in Spanish), which is currently 21 per cent on most goods. VAT refunds are available for purchases over €90.15 which will be taken outside the EU (see p136). You need to ask for a form, usually called a "cheque", to be filled in at the shop (note that not all stores participate in the scheme), then take it to be stamped at the customs counter at the airport, before getting a refund at a bureau de change or bank.

Dining

Catalan cuisine is widely regarded as one of the finest in the world, and Barcelona's eateries run the gamut from beachfront tapas bars and family-run taverns to chic, Michelin-starred gourmet restaurants.

The city's restaurants are increasingly offering a wider range of international cuisines, although Barcelona still lags behind most major European cities in this respect. Vegetarian restaurants have also proliferated in recent years, and there is now a much wider choice for vegetarians and vegans. Most restaurants offer a good value set-price lunch menu from Monday to Friday, a great way to try places that might otherwise be beyond your budget. The website **BCN Restaurantes** is useful for choosing and booking a place.

Restaurants usually open 1:30–3:30pm for lunch, and 8:30–11pm for dinner. If you want to dine earlier, tapas bars fill the gap and usually start serving at 6:30pm. Many places close on Sunday evenings.

Restaurants rarely offer child menus, but tapas provide an ideal solution if you're looking for smaller portions. Few restaurants have high chairs, so bring your own or ring ahead.

Cafés are an integral part of life here, and serve light meals and snacks along with coffee.

Where to Stay

There is something to suit all tastes and all budgets in Barcelona, whether you are looking for chic minimalism and plenty of services, or cosy chintz and a family-style welcome.

Accommodation falls into the following categories: hotels, rated between one and five stars; *hostals*, which are simple guest-houses often resembling hotels (not to be confused with youth hostels); B&Bs; holiday apartments; youth hostels, generally with dorms; and student residences, which offer inexpensive accommodation over the summer break. There are no campsites within the city, although you'll find a couple only a short bus or train trip from the city centre.

Rates are highest during peak travel periods such as Easter and Christmas, during trade shows, and often on Friday and Saturday nights. Prices drop significantly between mid-January and the start of Easter week, particularly in the self-catering holiday apartment category. Barcelona Turisme has comprehensive lists of

accommodation in all categories, and about 300 establishments can be booked through its website. **Barcelona Hotels** is the official booking website of the city's Hotel Association. **Hostelling International** helps you find and book hostel places. **BudgetPlaces**, **Oh-Barcelona**, **Airbnb**, **HostelWorld**, **Hotels.com** and **TripAdvisor** all have websites that help you choose and book accommodation, but it's always worth checking prices at the establishment itself before you make the booking online.

Barcelona is noisy, and it is worth packing earplugs, no matter in what category of hotel you are staying. Many places have darker but quieter interior rooms available; the brighter exterior rooms may have balconies but could suffer from street noise.

DIRECTORY

TRIPS AND TOURS

Art Bike Tour
w artbiketour.com

Bike Tours Barcelona
w biketoursbarcelona.com

Barcelona Turisme
w barcelonaturisme.com

Bus Turístic
w barcelonabusturistic.cat

Catalan Bird Tours
w catalanbirdtours.com

Cat Helicopters
w cathelicopters.com

GoCar
c 93 269 17 92
w gocarbarcelona.com

Las Golondrinas
w lasgolondrinas.com

Orsom Catamaran
w barcelona-orsom.com

Bright Side Tours
w brightsidetours.com

Ruta del Modernisme
w rutadelmodernisme.com

Segway Tours
w barcelonasegwaytour.com

SHOPPING

La Roca Village
w larocavillage.com

DINING

BCN Restaurantes
w bcnrestaurantes.com

WHERE TO STAY

Airbnb
w airbnb.com

Barcelona Hotels
w barcelonahotels.es

BudgetPlaces
w budgetplaces.com

Hostelling International
w hihostels.com

HostelWorld
w hostelworld.com

Hotels.com
w hotels.com

Oh-Barcelona
w oh-barcelona.com

TripAdvisor
w tripadvisor.com

Places to Stay

PRICE CATEGORIES
For a standard double room per night (with breakfast if included), including taxes and extra charges.

€ under €120   €€ €120–240   €€€ over €240

Luxury Hotels

Granados 83
MAP E2 ▪ C/Enric Granados 83 ▪ 93 492 96 70 ▪ www.hotel granados83.com ▪ €€
Rooms at this designer hotel are decorated with African zebrawood, chocolate brown leather and original pieces of Hindu and Buddhist art. Suites have private terraces that overlook a plunge pool. There is a restaurant, and a pretty rooftop pool with a fashionable bar.

ABaC Restaurant and Hotel
MAP B1 ▪ Av Tibidabo 1 ▪ 93 319 66 00 ▪ www. abacbarcelona.com ▪ €€€
This boutique hotel, set in a listed building, boasts luxury amenities perfectly suited for the smaller number of guests. The 17 gorgeous rooms are stylishly decorated in a contemporary, minimal style. There is a wellness spa with a hammam and Jacuzzi, plus a small garden. It also has one of the city's finest restaurants, ABaC, which earned its chef Jordi Cruz two Michelin stars.

Casa Camper
MAP L2 ▪ C/Elisabets 11 ▪ 93 342 62 80 ▪ www. casacamper.com ▪ €€€
A converted 19th-century mansion, this hotel is filled with innovative yet comfortable design touches. It has stylish rooms, a roof terrace, an extraordinary vertical garden and a free 24-hour bar. The Dos Palillos restaurant is run by Albert Raurich, former chef at El Bulli. Well-deserving of its Michelin star, it specializes in creative, tapas-style Asian dishes.

Fairmont Rey Juan Carlos I
Av Diagonal 661–671 ▪ 93 364 40 40 ▪ www. fairmont.com/barcelona ▪ €€€
This massive complex includes a vast private garden, two pools, a spa and conference facilities for 2,500 people. The spacious rooms are decorated in a contemporary style. The hotel's top floors offer unobstructed views of the city and mountains.

Grand Hotel Central
MAP E4 ▪ Via Laietana 30 ▪ 93 295 79 00 ▪ www. grandhotelcentral.com ▪ €€€
This large, elegant hotel has a great location close to the Barri Gòtic and El Born. It has accommodating staff, a fitness centre and a restaurant that serves desserts by the Michelin-starred chef Mey Hofmann. But the real highlight is the hotel's stunning rooftop infinity pool, which provides spectacular views of the city.

Hotel Arts Barcelona
MAP G5 ▪ C/Marina 19–21 ▪ 93 221 10 00 ▪ www.hotelarts barcelona.com ▪ €€€
This is the grande dame of the city's five-star hotels, is located mere steps from the sea, with large rooms and top-notch places to dine. Enoteca, run by Catalan chef Paco Pérez (of the Costa Brava's Miramar restaurant), offers imaginative Mediterranean cuisine and boasts two Michelin stars. The outoor pool on the first floor has fantastic views.

Hotel Omm
MAP E2 ▪ C/Rosselló 265 ▪ 93 445 40 00 ▪ www. hotelomm.es ▪ €€€
Designed by the award-winning Catalan architect Juli Capella, this is one of the hottest hotels in the city. The excellent Roca Moo restaurant (see p113), run by chef Juan Pretel, has a Michelin star and is overseen by the Roca brothers of the fabulous El Celler de Can Roca (see p131). The lobby Roca Bar is a great place for a bite any time of the day. There is a good spa and splendid views from the rooftop deck and pool.

Majestic Hotel and Spa
MAP E2 ▪ Pg de Gràcia 68 ▪ 93 492 22 44 ▪ www. hotelmajestic.es ▪ €€€
Faultless service and stately decor are the

hallmarks of this aptly named hotel. Exit through the reassuringly heavy brass-and-glass doors and you'll find yourself just a few steps from the *Modernista* gems of Eixample. The rooftop plunge pool has great views of the Barcelona cityscape and Gaudí's incredible masterpiece, the Sagrada Família.

El Palace Barcelona Hotel

MAP F3 ▪ Gran Via de les Corts Catalanes 668 ▪ 93 510 11 30 ▪ www.hotelpalace barcelona.com ▪ €€€

This deluxe hotel is synonymous with tradition and style, with its lovely 1919 Neo-Classical façade, grand public areas and excellent service. The Caelis restaurant, with one Michelin star, exudes 19th-century elegance and offers an innovative gourmet menu created by chef Romain Fornell.

W Barcelona

MAP E5 ▪ Pl de la Rosa dels Vents 1 ▪ 93 295 28 00 ▪ www.w-barcelona.com ▪ €€€

Popularly known as the Hotel Vela or the sail hotel, thanks to its nautically billowing form and location right next to the water, this lavishly appointed five-star option enjoys unparalleled sea views. With its massive floor-to-ceiling windows it is not hard to imagine you are at sea. The hotel has all the usual luxury extras, from a stunning rooftop pool and 7,500-sq-ft (700-sq-m) spa to six designer bars and restaurants.

Historical Hotels

Hotel Duquesa de Cardona

MAP M6 ▪ Pg Colón 12 ▪ 93 268 90 90 ▪ www.hduquesade cardona.com ▪ €€

The 16th-century home of the noble Cardona family used to host the royal court on its visits to the city. Now a stylish hotel, it combines the original structure with avant-garde decor and modern facilities. The rooftop terrace has a plunge pool and great views over the Port Vell area.

Hotel España

MAP L4 ▪ C/Sant Pau 9 ▪ 93 550 00 00 ▪ www.hotelespanya.com ▪ €€

This little gem of Catalan *Modernisme* is set in an 1850 building renovated in 1903 by *Modernista* architect Lluís Domènech i Montaner, artist Ramón Casas and sculptor Eusebi Arnau, who carved the splendid alabaster fireplace. There is a rooftop pool and solarium, and the Fonda España restaurant is run by Michelin-starred chef Martín Berasategui.

Praktik Rambla

MAP E3 ▪ Rambla de Catalunya 27 ▪ 93 343 66 90 ▪ www.hotelpraktik rambla.com ▪ €€

This centrally located budget hotel is set in a *Modernista* mansion. It combines traditional and avant-garde decor. The original tiling and carved woodwork from the 20th century make a striking contrast with the contemporary furnishings. The hotel has an outdoor terrace and also provides

free Wi-Fi. Book in advance as there are only a few rooms.

Casa Fuster

MAP E1 ▪ Pg de Gràcia 132 ▪ 93 255 30 00 ▪ www.hotelcasafuster.com ▪ €€€

Originally designed by Domènech i Montaner, whose works have been declared World Heritage Sites by the UNESCO. This hotel is one of the city's most prestigious and luxurious. The *Modernista* details have been retained, but elegantly fused with 21st-century amenities.

Gran Hotel La Florida

MAP B1 ▪ Ctra Vallvidrera al Tibidabo 83–93 ▪ 93 259 30 00 ▪ www.hotel laflorida.com ▪ €€€

Set in a *Modernista* villa high up in the hills in Tibidabo, this luxurious hotel has maintained its legendary views over the city since 1924, when it was built for Dr. Andreu, pharmaceutical entrepreneur and philanthropist. Its guests have included Ernest Hemingway, Princess Fabiola and the prince of Belgium. In 2001 it was meticulously and beautifully restored to its former glory.

Hotel 1898

MAP L2 ▪ La Rambla 109 ▪ 93 552 95 52 ▪ www.hotel1898.com ▪ €€€

This chic hotel has retained some of the building's original fittings, such as the early 20th-century revolving door, and added modern amenities, such as a swimming pool, a fitness centre and spa, and a good restaurant.

Hotel Claris

MAP E2 ▪ C/Pau Claris 150 ▪ 93 487 62 62 ▪ www.hotelclaris.com ▪ €€€

This 19th-century palace was once home to the Counts of Vedruna. It has a small Egyptian art museum, from the Old Kingdom to the Roman period, some objects from which also decorate the suites. Guests booking the Art Package get free admission to MNAC and the Museu Egipci (see p109), run by the owner.

Hotel Neri

MAP M3 ▪ C/Sant Sever 5 ▪ 93 304 06 55 ▪ www.hotelneri.com ▪ €€€

This 17th-century former palace at the heart of the Barri Gòtic offers an exclusive combination of history, the avant-garde and glamour. There is a library, a solarium and a roof terrace with views to the cathedral.

Mercer Hotel

MAP N4 ▪ C/Lledó 7 ▪ 93 310 74 80 ▪ www.mercerbarcelona.com ▪ €€€

This boutique hotel in the old part of town has 28 large, comfortable rooms. and the decor has a cutting-edge, designer feel to it. There are amazing views of the city from the swimming pool on the roof terrace, and a cocktail bar and restaurant.

Monument

MAP E2 ▪ Pg de Gràcia 75 ▪ 93 548 20 00 ▪ www.monumenthotel.com ▪ €€€

An old neo-Gothic palace right on the posh Passeig de Gràcia has been converted to a luxury hotel with an arty feel, including some bold contemporary design pieces. Guests can choose the street–facing rooms or the rear ones, which look out onto a typical Eixample courtyard.

Central Stays

chic&basic Born

MAP P4 ▪ C/Princesa 50 ▪ 93 295 46 52 ▪ www.chicandbasic.com ▪ €€

This 19th-century town house is a big hit with fashionistas. Rooms are minimalist with contemporary glass and steel bathrooms and colourful LED lights. Bike hire and activities such as stand-up paddle board are on offer, and there's a common area where you can chat with other guests.

Hotel Banys Orientals

MAP N4 ▪ C/Argenteria 37 ▪ 93 268 84 60 ▪ www.hotelbanysorientals.com ▪ €€

Behind the traditional frontage lies a modern, cosy hotel. Plusher suites are available in a separate building. The hotel's Senyor Parellada restaurant serves excellent Catalan cuisine, including speciality *bacalao* (cod) and *butifarra* (sausage). The cathedral, Museu Picasso and Barceloneta beach are close by.

Hotel Colón

MAP N3 ▪ Av de la Catedral 7 ▪ 93 301 14 04 ▪ hotelcolonbarcelona.es ▪ €€

A handsome, family-owned Barri Gòtic hotel, the Colón has traditional decor with mirrors and oil paintings throughout. The magnificent views of the cathedral and Plaça de la Seu are stunning. Hotel guests have included Sartre, Arata Isozaki and Joan Miró, who made this place his home in the 1960 and 70s.

Hotel Constanza

MAP F3 ▪ C/Bruc 33 ▪ 93 270 19 10 ▪ www.hotelconstanza.com ▪ €€

This elegant mid-sized hotel is near Eixample's main sights. Some of the stylish rooms come with terraces. The adjoining Bruc 33 restaurant serves homemade tapas and Mediterranean specialities.

Hotel Jazz

MAP L1 ▪ C/Pelai 3 ▪ 93 552 96 96 ▪ www.hoteljazz.com ▪ €€

The modern Hotel Jazz may not be the most characterful option, but it is centrally located and has several amenities, including a small rooftop pool. It is great value for money, and the friendly staff are always on hand to offer help and advice.

Hotel Soho Barcelona

MAP D3 ▪ Gran Vía Corts Catalanes 543 ▪ 93 552 96 10 ▪ www.hotelsohobarcelona.com ▪ €€

Top Spanish architect Alfredo Arribas designed this stylish, contemporary hotel. Located in the heart of Eixample, it's perfect for shopping, sightseeing and enjoying the nightlife. The rooftop pool has magnificent views.

Park Hotel

MAP F5 ▪ Av Marquès de l'Argentera 11 ▪ 93 319 60 00 ▪ www.parkhotelbarcelona.com ▪ €€

A 1950s design classic with a gorgeous

wrap-around staircase, the Park Hotel was refurbished by the original architect's son. Rooms are small but comfortably furnished, and some have balconies. It is located near the fashionable Born clubs and boutiques.

Room Mate Emma

MAP E2 ▪ C/Rosselló 205 ▪ 93 238 56 06 ▪ www. room-matehotels.com/ en/emma ▪ €€
A great option if you're looking for style on a budget, the Room Mate Emma offers compact but gorgeously designed bedrooms in the very centre of the city. There's no restaurant, but the staff can give recommendations.

Mandarin Oriental Barcelona

MAP E3 ▪ Pg de Gràcia 38–40 ▪ 93 151 88 88 ▪ www.mandarin oriental.com/barcelona ▪ €€€
This ultra-luxurious hotel boasts rooms overlooking either the iconic Passeig de Gràcia or the gorgeous interior gardens. It has a spa and a roof terrace with a splash pool. The gourmet restaurant. Moments, which serves exquisite Catalan cuisine and boasts two Michelin stars, is run by renowned chef Carme Ruscalleda of Sant Pau fame *(see p131)* – who has seven Michelin stars to her name – and her son Raül Balam.

Pullman Barcelona Skipper

MAP G6 ▪ Av Litoral 10 ▪ 93 221 65 65 ▪ www. pullman-barcelona-skipper.com ▪ €€€
Overlooking the sea close to the beach, the Pullman

is the perfect spot for a summer city break. Ideal for business travellers, it has all the facilities guests would expect of a five-star hotel. Weekend bargains are often available.

Mid-Priced Hotels

Circa 1905

MAP E2 ▪ C/Provença 286 ▪ 93 505 69 60 ▪ www. circa1905.com ▪ €€
This is one of a new breed of boutique B&Bs, and has just nine rooms (one with a private terrace) in a charming *Modernista* mansion. Furnished with a tasteful mix of antique and contemporary pieces, it has an elegant lounge where you can leaf through the books and enjoy a drink.

H10 Art Gallery

MAP E2 ▪ C/Enric Granados 62 ▪ 932 14 20 30 ▪ www.h10hotels.com ▪ €€
Colourful, contemporary and very chic, H10 Art Gallery has a beautiful interior patio and a roof-top terrace with a plunge pool. Rooms are bright and minimalist, and each floor draws inspiration from a different artist, from Miró to Lichtenstein. It's on one of Barcelona's prettiest streets, and has its own restaurant and café-bar.

Hotel Barcelona Catedral

MAP M3 ▪ C/Capellans 4 ▪ 93 304 22 55 ▪ www. barcelonacatedral.com ▪ €€
Enjoy phenomenal views over the Barri Gòtic from the roof terrace at this modern hotel, which also boasts a rooftop

plunge pool and a small fitness room. The guest rooms are spacious and bright, the service excellent, and the off-season prices a bargain. The hotel offers free bike hire, and conducts complimentary walking tours through the quarter on Wednesdays and Sundays.

Hotel Ciutat Vella

MAP L1 ▪ C/Tallers 66 ▪ 934 81 37 99 ▪ www. hotelciutatvella.com ▪ €€
Offering modern rooms decorated in warm colours, this great value option is located just a 5-minute walk from La Rambla. Some rooms have small terraces, and there is a plunge pool and sun deck on the roof.

Hotel Granvia

MAP F3 ▪ Gran Vía de les Corts Catalanes ▪ 642, 93 318 19 00 ▪ www.hotel granvia.com ▪ €€
Totally refurbished in 2013, this opulent late 19th-century mansion, built for a Barcelona philanthropist, has a domed stained-glass entrance, a fairy tale staircase and lavish stucco ceilings. The rooms have understated modern decor, and there is a charming hidden patio garden at the back.

Musik Boutique Hotel

MAP P3 ▪ C/Sant Pere Més Baix 62 ▪ 93 222 55 44 ▪ www.musik boutiquehotel.com ▪ €€
Close to the magnificent Palau de la Música, this small and welcoming hotel has a contemporary interior behind an 18th-century façade. The largest of the rooms have private terraces.

Praktik Vinoteca
MAP E3 ▪ C/Balmes 51
▪ 93 454 50 28 ▪ www.
hotelpraktikvinoteca.com
▪ €€
Ideal if you're looking
for style on a budget, this
wine-themed boutique
hotel in Eixample has
small but well-designed
rooms. You can enjoy a
wide range of local wines –
from the 900 or so on
display – in the elegant
and inviting lobby bar, and
there's also a miniature
terrace backed by plants.

Primero Primera
MAP B1 ▪ C/Doctor
Carulla 25–29 ▪ 93 417
56 00 ▪ www.primero
primera.com ▪ €€
This plush hotel in the
upmarket Sant Gervasi
area combines vintage
chic with contemporary
sophistication. There's a
cosy lounge with an open
fire and leather armchairs
and a romantic little
garden with a small
pool and sun loungers.

Villa Emilia
MAP C3 ▪ C/Calàbria 115
▪ 93 252 52 85 ▪ www.
hotelvillaemilia.com ▪ €€
Slightly off the beaten
track, but close to the
hip Sant Antoni neighbourhood, which is packed
with bars and boutiques,
this friendly hotel offers
stylish rooms and a roof
terrace for barbecues
in summer and cocktails
under heaters in winter.
The lobby bar has regular
jazz concerts.

Violeta Boutique
MAP F3 & N1 ▪ C/Caspe
38 ▪ 93 302 81 58 ▪ violet
aboutique.com ▪ €€
Each of the spacious
rooms at this lovely
guesthouse has been
individually decorated,
and guests can sit out
on a pretty balcony with
a drink or the newspaper.
They also offer a small
apartment which has its
own kitchen and terrace.

Budget Hotels

Casa Bella Gràcia
MAP F1 ▪ C/Sant Agustí
4 ▪ 93 667 78 41 ▪ www.
casabellagracia.com ▪ €
Located in a beautiful
building, this stylish hotel
has a communal terrace
and modern rooms. There
are no dining facilities, but
there are plenty of places
to eat and drink nearby.
Guests are given an
entrance code on booking,
as there is no reception.

chic&basic Zoo
MAP Q4 ▪ Pg Picasso 22
▪ 93 295 46 52 ▪ www.
chicandbasic.com ▪ €
Part of the chic&basic
chain, this small hotel
is located in a historic
building in the heart of
the Born district, opposite
Parc de la Ciutadella. The
largest rooms have bal-
conies facing the park.

El Balcon del Born
MAP P5 ▪ C/Rera Palau 2
▪ 63 452 45 05 (mobile)
www.elbalcondelborn-
barcelona.com ▪ €
In the fashionable Born
district, this guesthouse
has 10 delightful rooms
(private or shared bath-
rooms). Each is individually
decorated and has its
own balcony. Book early.

El Jardí
MAP M3 ▪ Pl Sant Josep
Oriol 1 ▪ 93 301 59 00
▪ www.eljardi-barcelona.
com ▪ €
In the snug heart of the
Barri Gòtic, this hostel
has simple, spotless en
suite rooms done up in
light wood and cool
colours. The bright breakfast room has balconies
overlooking the square.

Hostal Goya
MAP N1 ▪ C/Pau Claris
74 ▪ 93 302 25 65 ▪ www.
hostalgoyabarcelona.
com ▪ €
This well-run hostel was
established in 1952. The
rooms are bright and
modern, with some
designer touches. Most
have en suite bathrooms;
some have air conditioning.

Hostal Oliva
MAP E3 ▪ Pg de Gràcia
32 ▪ 93 488 01 62 ▪ No
credit cards ▪ www.
hostaloliva.com ▪ €
From the the individually
wrapped soaps to the
lovely vintage elevator,
this cheerful, family-
run hostel is one of the
city's best. The beautiful
Modernista building has
airy rooms, some with
en suite bathrooms.

Market
MAP D3 ▪ Comte Borrell
68 ▪ 93 325 12 05 ▪ www.
hotelmarketbarcelona.
com ▪ €
Close to the *Modernista*
Sant Antoni market, the
rooms in this stylish hotel
have an oriental feel, with
glossy lacquered wood
and a red, white and black
colour scheme. Book well
in advance.

Sol y k
MAP M5 ▪ C/Cervantes
2 ▪ 93 318 81 48
▪ www.solyk.es ▪ €
A budget option in the
heart of the Barri Gòtic.
A handful of individually
decorated rooms with
mosaic headboards and

original art set the Sol y k apart from other guest-houses. Some rooms have en suites.

Hotel Acta Mimic

MAP K5 ▪ C/Arc del Teatre 58 ▪ 93 329 94 50 ▪ www. hotel-mimic.com ▪ €€
Close to La Rambla, this hotel is set in a building that once housed a theatre. The rooms are well-lit and airy, with large windows and sleek, modern decor. Guests can relax on the sunbeds arranged on the roof terrace, which doubles as a solarium with a view over the old town and the port.

Hotel Brummell

MAP 5C ▪ C/Nou de la Rambla 174 ▪ 93 125 86 22 ▪ www.hotel brummell.com ▪ €€
A stylish little charmer in lively Poble Sec, this hotel has a rooftop sun deck and plunge pool to go with the contem-porarily styled rooms. Complimentary yoga classes, a sauna and a great little café make it the perfect city oasis.

Campsites and Aparthotels

Aparthotel Atenea

C/Joan Güell 207–211 ▪ 93 490 66 40 ▪ www. aparthotelatenea. com ▪ €
Designed with business travellers in mind, this top-notch aparthotel is sited near the business and financial district around upper Diagonal. Rooms are spacious and well equipped, and there are several conference rooms and a 24-hour laundry service.

Aparthotel Bertran

C/de Bertran 150 ▪ 93 212 75 50 ▪ www. bertran-hotel.com ▪ €
This aparthotel has generous studios and apartments (many with balconies), a rooftop swimming pool, a small gym and 24-hour laun-dry service. Breakfast is served in your apartment.

Cala Llevadó Ctra

Ctra GI-682 km 18.9, Tossa de Mar ▪ 97 234 03 14 ▪ www.calallevado. com ▪ €
This well-kept, eco-friendly campsite is on the Costa Brava near the beautiful beach town of Tamariu. It is just 200 m (656 ft) from the beach and within walking distance of the town for bars, restaurants and grocery shops. The campsite has a pictur-esque location by the sea, with palm-shaded pitches for tents. Great for families.

Camping Barcelona

Ctra N-II, km 650, 8 km (5 miles) E of Mataró ▪ 93 790 47 20 ▪ Closed Nov–Mar ▪ www.camping barcelona.com ▪ €
Located 28 km (17 miles) north of Barcelona, this is set right next to a small beach and close to several larger ones. Bungalows are available to rent as are pitches.

Camping Globo Rojo

Ctra N-II km 660, 9, Canet de Mar ▪ 93 794 11 43 ▪ Closed Oct–Mar ▪ www. globo-rojo.com ▪ €
Close to the beaches of Canet de Mar, Globo Rojo offers pitches, mobile homes, bungalows and other accommodation units. There is a pool, tennis court and football

pitch. Great for kids. Direct bus and train to Barcelona.

Camping Masnou Barcelona

C/Camil Fabra 33 (N-II, km 663), El Masnou ▪ 93 555 15 03 ▪ Credit card minimum €100 ▪ www.campingmasnou barcelona.com ▪ €
This family-owned camp-site is located 11 km (7 miles) north of Barcelona and close to the El Masnou train station, which is a 20-minute journey from the city. The campsite faces the sea and has a small beach close by. They offer shaded pitches as well as rooms, and facil-ities include a swimming pool, a supermarket and a terrace bar with Wi-Fi.

Camping Roca Grossa

Ctra N-II km 665, Calella ▪ 93 769 12 97 ▪ Closed Oct–Mar ▪ www.roca grossa.com ▪ €
Positioned between the mountains and the sea, this modern campsite has good installations and access to the nearby beach. It has a large swimming pool, a restau-rant and bar and is only 1 km (0.6 mile) from the lively resort of Calella. Both pitches and bun-galows are available.

Camping Sitges

Ctra Comarcal C-246a, km 38, Sitges ▪ 93 894 10 80 ▪ Closed mid-Oct–mid-March ▪ www. campingsitges.com ▪ €
This is a small, well-kept campsite with a swimming pool, playground and a supermarket. It is located 2 km (1 mile) south of Sitges, and close to its renowned beaches.

For a key to hotel price categories see p142

Citadines
MAP L2 ▪ La Rambla 122
▪ 93 270 11 11 ▪ www.
citadines.com ▪ €€
If you're smitten with
the city, try an aparthotel for
a longer stay. This one
on La Rambla has well-
appointed studios and
small apartments with
a kitchenette, iron and
CD stereo. The rooftop
terrace has beach chairs
and showers and is just
the spot to unwind.

Oh-Barcelona
93 467 37 79 ▪ www.
oh-barcelona.com ▪ €€
This company has a huge
number of apartments
in and around the city.
Prices for a one-bedroom
apartment range from
€55 to €160 per night.

Hostels and Student Residences

Be Dream Hostel Barcelona
Av Alfonso XIII 28b,
Badalona ▪ 93 399 14 20
▪ www.behostels.com/
dream ▪ €
A 20-minute metro ride
from the city centre, but
close to the beaches, this
hostel is well priced, with
rooms and dorms sleeping
between 2 and 12 guests.
Kitchen and laundry
facilities are included.

Equity Point Centric Hostel
MAP E3 ▪ Pg de Gràcia
33 ▪ 93 231 20 45 ▪ www.
equity-point.com ▪ €
Housed in a renovated
Modernista building, this
hostel has large dorms,
as well as single and
double rooms with private
facilities. There is a common room with a bar, free
Internet and satellite TV.

Equity Point Gothic Hostel
MAP N4 ▪ C/Vigatans 5
▪ 93 231 20 45 ▪ www.
equity-point.com ▪ €
This bright, well-run,
central hostel has dorm
rooms sleeping 6 to 18.
Breakfast is included
in the price and there
is free 24-hour Internet
access. All rooms have
air conditioning.

Feetup Garden House Hostel
C/ d'Hedilla 58 ▪ 93 427
24 79 ▪ www.feetup
hostels.com ▪ €
This friendly hostel is
located on the outskirts
of the city, near Gaudí's
beautiful Park Güell. It's
only a 15-minute metro
ride into the centre of
town. There is a lovely
garden and roof terrace,
and a relaxed vibe.

INOUT Hostel
▪ C/Major del Rectornet 2,
Vallvidrera ▪ 93 280 09 85
▪ www.inouthostel.com ▪ €
Located a 12-minute train
ride from the city centre
in the forest-filled enclave
Vallvidrera, INOUT Hostel
is an admirable enterprise
that provides employment
for disabled people. Rooms
accommodate four to ten
people. There are sports
facilities and a pool.

Itaca Hostel
MAP N3 ▪ C/Ripoll 21
▪ 93 301 97 51 ▪ www.
itacahostel.com ▪ €
Located in the heart of the
Barri Gòtic Quarter, this is
a clean hostel with space
for 30 guests in double
rooms, dorms (for up to
6 people) and apartments.
Bedding and lockers are
included in the price and
there is Wi-Fi available
in the main building.

Kabul Hostel
MAP L4 ▪ Pl Reial 17
▪ 93 318 51 90
▪ www.kabul.es ▪ €
Kabul is a favourite with
young backpackers, so
it's often full (and noisy).
Dorm rooms, all with air
conditioning and some
with balconies, sleep 4–
20 people. There's free
Internet access, lockers,
a laundry, and a small
café open during the day.

Mambo Tango
MAP C4 ▪ C/Poeta
Cabanyes 23 ▪ 93 442 51
64 ▪ www.hostelmambo
tango.com ▪ €
Former travellers Toto
and Marino are behind
this warm and welcoming
hostel. It has dorms for
four, six, eight and nine
people, breakfast and
sheet-hire are included
in the price, and extras
include complimentary
hot drinks and fruit. Party
animals are actively dis-
couraged, so you can count
on getting a good night's
sleep during your stay.

Pars Tailor's Hostel
MAP D3 ▪ C/Sepulveda
146 ▪ 93 250 56 84 ▪
www.parshostels.com ▪ €
A mother-and-daughter
team run this charming
hostel, which features
vintage interiors designed
to evoke a Parisian tailor's
in the 1930s. The well-
equipped air-conditioned
dorms have lockers.
There is a terrace, lounge
and many free activities.

Sant Jordi Apartment Sagrada Família
MAP E2 ▪ C/Freser 5
▪ 93 446 05 17 ▪ www.
santjordihostels.com ▪ €
The Sant Jordi group's
most comfortable accom-
modation in Barcelona,

this offers relaxed, homely living. Each unit has a fully equipped kitchen, living room and one or two bathrooms, plus a private room, a double room and a dorm. Whole apartments can also be rented – great for families and large groups.

Getaways Beyond Barcelona

Ca l'Aliu
C/Roca 6, Peratallada, 12 km (7.5 miles) NW of Palafrugell ▪ 97 263 40 61 ▪ www.calaliu.com ▪ €€
In the tiny medieval town of Peratallada stands this restored 18th-century *casa rural*. The cosy, comfortable rooms have antique furniture and are all en suite. The owners will lend you bikes, and the town and surrounding villages offer a range of sporting activities.

Hostal Sa Tuna
Pg de Ancora 6, Platja Sa Tuna, 5 km N of Begur ▪ 97 262 21 98 ▪ Closed Oct–Mar ▪ www.hostal satuna.com ▪ €€
Take in the sea views from your terrace at this five-room, family-run hotel on the pretty Platja Sa Tuna. The restaurant serves excellent Catalan cuisine and breakfast is included in the price of the room.

Hotel Aigua Blava
Platja de Fornells, Begur ▪ 97 262 20 58 ▪ Closed mid-Oct–late Mar ▪ www. hotelaiguablava.com ▪ €€
This coastal institution, perched atop rugged cliffs overlooking the sea, is run by the fourth generation of the same family. Many of the rooms – each

individually decorated – have splendid of the Mediterranean. There's a large outdoor pool and breakfast is included in the price. Apartments are also available.

Hotel Aiguaclara
C/Sant Miquel 2, Begur ▪ 97 262 29 05 ▪ www. hotelaiguaclara.com ▪ €€
This charming hotel, set in a whitewashed 1866 colonial villa in the centre of town, was built by a Begur "indiano" – a local nickname for those who made their fortunes in Cuba in the early 19th century. The beautiful rooms are a mix of contemporary furnishings and original features. The wonderful restaurant and outstanding service make this the ideal place for a romantic break.

Hotel Blau Mar
C/Farena 36, Llafranc ▪ 97 261 00 55 ▪ hotelblau marllafranc.com ▪ €€
A delightful hotel in a seaside village, Blau Mar has traditionally decorated rooms (most with terraces), lovely gardens and a pool with views out to sea. There are several clifftop walks and coves to explore in the vicinity.

Hotel Can Barrina
Ctra de Palautordera al Montseny, km 12, 670, Montseny ▪ 93 847 30 65 ▪ www. canbarrina.com/ en ▪ €€
An 18th-century farmhouse set in the hills of Montseny, is now a charming boutique hotel with an excellent restaurant. Comfortable rooms, extensive gardens and an outdoor pool make it the perfect place to relax.

Hotel Historic
C/Belmirall 4a, Girona ▪ 97 222 35 83 ▪ www. hotelhistoric.com ▪ €€
Located in the heart of the old quarter, just around the corner from the cathedral, this is a good base for exploring Girona. Guests have the option of choosing either the rooms or the self-catering apartments.

Parador de Tortosa
Castillo de la Zuda, Tortosa ▪ 97 744 44 50 ▪ www.parador.es ▪ €€
Looming over the town of Tortosa is the ancient Arab Castillo de la Zuda, within which this *parador* is housed. The decor is suitably old-world, with dark-wood furniture and antique fixtures. The view of the countryside and mountains is superb.

Val de Neu
C/Perimetrau s/n ▪ 97 363 50 00 ▪ www.hotel baqueiravaldeneu.com ▪ Closed May–Sep ▪ €€
Perhaps the most sumptuous ski hotel in the chic resort of Baqueria Beret, Val de Neu is located right next to the slopes. Among the five-star amenities are a spa, a pool and an array of restaurants.

El Castell de la Ciutat
Crta N-260, km 229, La Seu d'Urgell ▪ 97 335 00 00 ▪ www.hotelelcastell. com ▪ €€€
Located right next to a 16th-century castle, this hotel offers refined luxury in the heart of the Pyrenees. There are a couple of restaurants, a spa, beautiful gardens, pools, and wonderful views of the mountains.

For a key to hotel price categories see p142

General Index

Acknowledgments

The Authors
Travel writer, reporter and editor AnneLise Sorensen is half-Catalan and has lived and worked in Barcelona. She has penned her way across four continents, contributing to guidebooks, magazines and newspapers.

Ryan Chandler is a writer and journalist who has been working in Barcelona for over ten years. He previously worked as Barcelona correspondent for the Spanish magazine *The Broadsheet*.

Additional contributor
Mary-Ann Gallagher

Publishing Director Georgina Dee

Publisher Vivien Antwi

Design Director Phil Ormerod

Editorial Ankita Awasthi-Tröger, Michelle Crane, Rachel Fox, Fíodhna Ní Ghríofa, Freddie Marriage, Scarlett O'Hara, Sally Schafer, Jackie Staddon, Christine Stroyan

Design Tessa Bindloss, Richard Czapnik

Picture Research Phoebe Lowndes, Susie Peachey, Ellen Root, Oran Tarjan

Cartography Subhashree Bharti, Tom Coulson, Martin Darlison, Simonetta Giori, Suresh Kumar, Casper Morris

DTP Jason Little, George Nimmo, Azeem Siddiqui

Production Linda Dare

Factchecker Paula Canal

Proofreader Kate Berens

Indexer Hilary Bird

Illustrator Chris Orr & Associates, Lee Redmond

Commissioned Photography
Max Alexander, Departure Lounge/Ella Milroy, Departure Lounge/Paul Young, Joan Farre, Heidi Grassley, Alex Robinson, Rough Guides/Ian Aitken, Rough Guides/Chris Christoforou, Rough Guides/ Tim Kavenagh.

Revisions
Kate Berens, Mary-Ann Gallagher, Aishwarya Gosain, Bharti Karakoti, Sumita Khatwani, Alison McGill, George Nimmo, Adrian Potts, Ankita Sharma, Lucy Sienkowska, Rituraj Singh, Hollie Teague, Richa Verma, Penny Walker, Suzanne Wales.

First edition created by Departure Lounge, London

Picture Credits
The publisher would like to thank the following for their kind permission to reproduce their photographs:
Key: a-above; b-below/bottom; c-centre; f-far; l-left; r-right; t-top

123RF.com: Lucian Milasan 7cr; Luciano Mortula 7tr; Tagstock Japan 14ca.

4Corners: SIME/Olimpio Fantuz 1c; SIME/Pietro Canali 4cla, 24–5.

Acontaluz: Acontaluz 123br.

Alamy Images: age fotostock 2tr, 36–7, 58tl, / Alfred Abad 108cl, /Mike Finn-Kelcey 130tl, / Rafael Campillo 66b; Juan Bautista 98cr; Robert Dodge 61tr; Peter Erik Forsberg 47bl; Manfred Gottschalk 16–17tc; Hemis 85cl; Hemis /Patrice Hauser 110tl; John Henshall 27tl; LOOK Die Bildagentur der Fotografen GmbH/Juergen Richter 43tr; Stefano Politi Markovina 68bl; Giuseppe Masci 55tr; National Geographic Image Collection 60br; Cisco Pelay 79cl; Ingolf Pompe 52 60tl; Radharc Images 12tr; Sam Bloomberg-Rissman 69b; Marek Stepan 91tr; Gregory Wrona 78cb.

Hotel Arts Barcelona: David Monfil 104cr.

AWL Images: Sabine Lubenow 2tl, 4b, 8–9; Stefano Politi Markovina 56–7, 114–5.

Bar Almirall: Bar Almirall 92tl.

Bar del Pla: Bar del Pla 84br.

Bobby Gin: Pau Esculies 122tl.

Boo: 120tl.

BOO Restaurant & Beach Club: BOO Restaurant & Beach Club 104tl.

Bridgeman Images: Museu d'Art Contemporani de Barcelona © ADAGP, Paris and DACS, London 2015. Homea, 1974 Eduardo Arranz Bravo (b.1941) 34br; Museu Picasso, Barcelona © Succession Picasso/ DACS, London 2015 Harlequin, 1917, Pablo Picasso (1881–1973) 31tll, Seated Man, 1917, Pablo Picasso (1881–1973) 31tr; Menu from 'Els Quatre Gats', 1899, Pablo Picasso (1881–1973) 30bc, Las Meninas, No.30, 1957, Pablo Picasso (1881–1973) 30–31cb.

Comunikare: Comunikare 110cb.

Corbis: Guido Cozzi 67cl; Design Pics/Axiom Photographic 4crb, /Ken Welsh 39tr; Gavin Jackson 35cb; Heritage Images 15tl; JAI/Stefano Politi Markovina 72tl, 92br; Jean-Pierre Lescourret 34bl; René Mattes 41tr; Charlie Pérez 54tl; Sylvain Sonnet 18–19c; Sandro Vannini 16c; Wally McNamee 39bl.

Cafe de l'Opera: Cafe de l'Opera 64bl.

Dorling Kindersley: Museu d'Art Contemporani, Barcelona © Foundation Antoni Tapies, Barcelone/VEGAP, Madrid and DACS, London 2015 Deconstructed bed (1992–3) 35tl; Courtesy of the Palau de la Musica Catalana 33tl.

Dreamstime.com: Alexvaneekelen 80tl; Steve Allen 45br, 87bl, 95tr; Danilo Ascione 48tr; Christian Bertrand 55clb, 73tr; Daniel Sanchez Blasco 87tr; Brandon Bourdages 100tr; Byelikova 124tl; Catalby 3tr, 28cla; Charles03 50tl; Dennis Dolkens 119bl; Dinozzaver 44b; Dnaveh 53c; Edufoto 6cla; Ego450 23tl; Elxeneize 16bl, 116tr; Alexandre Fagundes De Fagundes 41clb; Fazon1 10bl, Fotoember 26cb, 26–7c, Gelia 125tr; Iakov Filimonov 43clb, 52clb, 72br; Jackf 50cb, 51b, 70br, 107tr, 126tr, 126–7b; Javarman 4cr, 32cl; Jiawangkun 104tl; Karsol 12–13c, 17cr; Kemaltaner 4t; Karol Kozlowski 49tr; Kyolshin 14bl; Lanaufoto 129c; Lavendertime 18cl; Lisja 11tl, Loflo69 128br; Mark52 32–3c, Carlos Soler Martinez 46bl, 73cla, Alberto Masnovo 42t; Masterlu 15b; Matteocozzi 40ca; Miff32 71cl; Lucian Milasan 96b; Miluxian 22br; Miskolin 118t; Mkoudis 11crb; Luciano Mortula 45tl, 68tr; Juan Moyano 40bl, 46t, 48b, 102–3b; Nito100 70tl, 108tr; Andrey Omelyanchuk 88bl; Pat@xs4all.nl 22cla; Pathastings 63tr; Marek Poplawski 102tl; Rquemades 4cl; Santirf 108–9b; Victor Zastol`skiy 97cl; Ron Sumners 65tr; Toniflap 48c, 76tl; Typhoonski 77tr; Vichie81 12bc; Vitalyedush 4clb, 95b; Dmitry Volkov 89bl; Yuri4u80 22–3c; Yuryz 27bl.

El Celler de Can Roca: Joan Pujol-Creus 131crb.

Escriba: Escriba 81cla.

Galeria Cosmo: Galeria Cosmo 112t.

Getty Images: Culture Club 38c; Jean-Pierre Lescourre 71tr; Popperfoto 39cla; David Ramos 61clb; Redferns/Jordi Vidal 58crb; Sylvain Sonnet 10tr.

Granja Dulcinea: Granja Dulcinea 65clb.

Harlem Jazz Club: 54br, 83clb.

Imanol Ossa: 90c.

iStockphoto.com: kanuman 3tl, 74–5; MasterLu 5tr, 132–133.

Fundacio Joan Miro: © Successió Miró / ADAGP, Paris and DACS London 2015 11cra, Catalan Peasant by Moonlight 28bc, Tapis de la Fundacio 28–9c, Sculpture on the Terrace Garden at Fundacio Joan Miro in Barcelona 29tl.

L'Arca: 81br.

La Manual Alpargatera: 81tc.

La Mar Salada: 105br.

Le Standard: 121br.

Bar Lobo: Olga Planas 64tr.

Moments/Mandarin Oriental Hotel Group: George Apostolidis 113br.

Marmalade : Duda Bussolin 93cra.

Dry Martini : Javier de las Muelas 111br.

Metro: 60c.

Milk Bar & Bistro: Duda Bussolin 82bl.

Museu d'Art Contemporani de Barcelona (MACBA): Rafael Vargas 11bl, 34–35c.

Polaroids: Meg Diaz 83tr.

Razzmatazz: 59b.

Photo Scala, Florence: © Succession Picasso/ DACS, London 2015 Painting of Margot, or Waiting, 1901 Pablo Picasso 11c.

SuperStock: DeAgostini Painting of Our Lady of Councilors 1445, by Lluis Dalmau 10br; Fine Art Images The Virgin of Humility (Madonna dell' Umilita) Angelico, Fra Giovanni, da Fiesole (ca. 1400–1455) 20bl; Hemis.fr 33br; Iberfoto /National Art Museum of Catalonia /Painting of The Minuet. 1756. Bequest of Francesc Camb by TIEPOLO, Giovanni Domenico (1727–1804) 20cr; /Ramon Casas and Pere Romeu on a Tandem. 1897. by CASAS i CARBO, Ram—n (1866–1932) 21tl, /Ducat with the image of Philip V (1703). Coin 21cra; JTB Photo 32br; Joan Miro Foundation, Barcelona © Successió Miró/ADAGP, Paris and DACS London 2015. Sculpture gallery display 29cr; Picasso Museum, Barcelona © Succession Picasso/DACS, London 2015 Dwarf Dancer (Nana) (Danseuse Naine (La Nana)) 1901 Pablo Picasso (1881–1973 /Spanish) 30cl.

La Taverna del Clinic: 62t.

The Tatami Room: 99tr.

Tinta Invisible: 90bl.

Windsor: 62br.

Cover

Front and spine – **Picfair.com:** Sharon Whishwilson.
Back – **4Corners:** SIME / Pietro Canali t.

Pull out map cover

Picfair.com: Sharon Whishwilson.

All other images are: © Dorling Kindersley. For further information see www.dkimages.com.

As a guide to abbreviations in visitor information:
Adm = admission charge; **D** = dinner; **L** = lunch.

Penguin Random House

Printed and bound in China

First American Edition, 2002
Published in the United States by
DK Publishing, 345 Hudson Street,
New York, New York 10014

Copyright 2002, 2018 © Dorling Kindersley Limited

A Penguin Random House Company

18 19 20 21 10 9 8 7 6 5 4 3 2 1

Reprinted with revisions 2004, 2005, 2006, 2007, 2008, 2009, 2010, 2011, 2012, 2013, 2014, 2016 (twice), 2017, 2018

Published in Great Britain by Dorling Kindersley Limited.

A catalog record for this book is available from the Library of Congress.

ISSN 1479-344X
ISBN 978-1-4654-7149-9

MIX
Paper from responsible sources
FSC™ C018179

SPECIAL EDITIONS OF DK TRAVEL GUIDES

English-Catalan Phrase Book

In an Emergency

Help!	Auxili!	ow-gzee-lee
Stop!	Pareu!	pah-reh-oo
Call a doctor!	Telefoneu un metge!	teh-leh-fon-eh-oo oon meh-djuh
Call an ambulance!	Telefoneu una ambulància!	teh-leh-fon-eh-oo oo-nah ahm-boo-lahn-see-ah
Call the police!	Telefoneu la policia	teh-leh-fon-eh-oo lah poh-lee-see-ah
Call the fire brigade!	Telefoneu els bombers!	teh-leh-fon-eh-oo uhlz boom-behs
Where is the nearest telephone?	On és el telèfon més proper?	on-ehs uhl tuh-leh fon mehs proo-peh
Where is the nearest hospital?	On és l'hospital més proper?	on-ehs looss-pee-tahl mehs proo-peh

Communication Essentials

Yes	Sí	see
No	No	noh
Please	Si us plau	sees plah-oo
Thank you	Gràcies	grah-see-uhs
Excuse me	Perdoni	puhr-thoh-nee
Hello	Hola	oh-lah
Goodbye	Adéu	ah-they-oo
Good night	Bona nit	bo-nah neet
Morning	El matí	uhl mah-tee
Afternoon	La tarda	lah tahr-thuh
Evening	El vespre	uhl vehs-pruh
Yesterday	Ahir	ah-ee
Today	Avui	uh-voo-ee
Tomorrow	Demà	duh-mah
Here	Aquí	uh-kee
There	Allà	uh-lyah
What?	Què?	keh
When?	Quan?	kwahn
Why?	Per què?	puhr keh
Where?	On?	ohn

Useful Phrases

How are you?	Com està?	kom uhs-tah
Very well, thank you.	Molt bé, gràcies.	mol beh grah-see-uhs
Pleased to meet you.	Molt de gust.	mol duh goost
See you soon.	Fins aviat.	feenz uhv-yat
Where is/are ..?	On és/són?	ohn ehs/sohn
How far is it to?	Quants metres/ kilòmetres hi ha d'aquí a ...?	kwahnz meh-truhs/kee-loh-muh-truhs yah dah-kee uh
Which way to ...?	Per on es va a ...?	puhr on uhs bah ah
Do you speak English?	Parla anglès?	par-luh an-glehs
I don't understand.	No l'entenc.	noh luhn-teng
Could you speak more slowly, please?	Pot parlar més a poc a poc, si us plau?	pot par-lah mehs pok uh pok sees plah-oo
I'm sorry.	Ho sento.	oo sehn-too

Useful Words

big	gran	gran
small	petit	puh-teet
hot	calent	kah-len
cold	fred	fred
good	bo	boh
bad	dolent	doo-len
enough	bastant	bahs-tan
well	bé	beh
open	obert	oo-behr
closed	tancat	tan-kat
left	esquerra	uhs-kehr-ruh
right	dreta	dreh-tuh
straight on	recte	rehk-tuh
near	a prop	uh prop
far	lluny	lyoonyuh
up/over	a dalt	uh dahl
down/under	a baix	uh bah-eeshh
early	aviat	uhv-yat
late	tard	tahrt
entrance	entrada	uhn-trah-thuh
exit	sortida	soor-tee-thuh
toilet	lavabos/ serveis	luh-vah-boos sehr-beh-ees
more	més	mess
less	menys	menyees

Shopping

How much does this cost?	Quant costa això?	kwahn kost ehs-shoh
I would like ...	M'agradaria ...	muh-grah-thuh-ree-ah
Do you have?	Tenen?	tehn-un
I'm just looking, thank you	Només estic mirant, gràcies.	noo-mess ehs-teek mee-rahn grah-see-uhs
Do you take credit cards?	Accepten targes de crèdit?	ak-sehp-tuhn tahr-zhuhs duh kreh-deet
What time do you open?	A quina hora obren?	ah keen-uh oh-ruh oh-bruhn
What time do you close?	A quina hora tanquen?	ah keen-uh oh -ruh tan-kuhn
This one.	Aquest	ah-ket
That one.	Aquell	ah-kehl
That's fine.	Està bé.	uhs-tah beh
expensive	car	kahr
cheap	bé de preu/barat	beh thuh preh-oo/bah-rat
size (clothes)	talla/mida	tah-lyah/mee-thuh
size (shoes)	número	noo-mehr-oo
white	blanc	blang
black	negre	neh-gruh
red	vermell	vuhr-mel
yellow	groc	grok
green	verd	behrt
blue	blau	blah-oo
antique store	antiquari/botiga d'antiguitats	an-tee-kwah-ree/boo-tee-gah/dan-tee-ghee-tats
bakery	el forn	uhl forn
bank	el banc	uhl bang

book store	la llibreria	lah lyee-bruh-ree-ah
butcher's	la carnisseria	lah kahr-nee-suh-ree-uh
pastry shop	la pastisseria	lah pahs-tee-suh-ree-uh
chemist's	la farmàcia	lah fuhr-mah-see-ah
fishmonger's	la peixateria	lah peh-shuh-tuh-ree-uh
greengrocer's	la fruiteria	lah froo-ee-tuh-ree-uh
grocer's	la botiga de queviures	lah boo-tee-guh duh keh-vee-oo-ruhs
hairdresser's	la perruqueria	lah peh-roo-kuh-ree-uh
market	el mercat	uhl muhr-kat
newsagent's	el quiosc de premsa	uhl kee-ohsk duh prem-suh
post office	l'oficina de correus	loo-fee-see-nuh duh koo-reh-oos
shoe store	la sabateria	lah sah-bah-tuh-ree-uh
supermarket	el supermercat	uhl soo-puhr-muhr-kat
travel agency	l'agència de viatges	la-jen-see-uh duh vee-ad-juhs

Sightseeing

art gallery	la galeria d'art	lah gah-luh-ree-yuh dart
cathedral	la catedral	lah kuh-tuh-thrahl
church	l'església	luhz-gleh-zee-uh
garden	el jardí	uhl zhahr-dee
library	la biblioteca	lah bee-blee-oo-teh-kuh
museum	el museu	uhl moo-seh-oo
tourist information office	l'oficina de turisme	loo-fee-see-nuh thuh too-reez-muh
town hall	l'ajuntament	luh-djoon-tuh-men
closed for holiday	tancat per vacances	tan-kat puhr bah-kan-suhs
bus station	l'estació d'autobusos	luhs-tah-see-oh dow-toh-boo-zoos
railway station	l'estació de tren	luhs-tah-see-oh thuh tren

Staying in a Hotel

Do you have a vacant room?	¿Tenen una habitació lliure?	teh-nuhn oo-nuh ah-bee-tuh-see-oh lyuh-ruh
double room with double bed	habitació doble amb llit de matrimoni	ah-bee-tuh-see-oh doh-bluh am lyeet duh mah-tree-moh-nee
twin room	habitació amb dos llits/amb llits individual	ah-bee-tuh-see-oh am dohs lyeets/am lyeets in-thee-vee-thoo-ahls
single room	habitació individual	ah-bee-tuh-see-oh een-dee-vee-thoo-ahl
room with	habitació	ah-bee-tuh-see-oh
a bath	amb bany	am bahnyuh
shower	dutxa	doo-chuh
porter	el grum	uhl groom
key	la clau	lah klah-oo
I have a reservation	Tinc una habitació reservada	ting oo-nuh ah-bee-tuh-see-oh reh-sehr-vah-thah

Eating Out

Have you got a table for…	Tenen taula per…?	teh-nuhn tow-luh puhr
I would like to reserve a table.	Voldria reservar una taula.	vool-dree-uh reh-sehr-vahr oo-nuh tow-luh
The bill please	El compte, si us plau.	uhl kohm-tuh sees plah-oo
I am a vegetarian	Sóc vegetarià/vegetariana	sok buh-zhuh-tuh-ree-ah/buh-zhuh-tuh-ree-ah-nah
waitress	cambrera	kam-breh-ruh
waiter	cambrer	kam-breh
menu	la carta	lah kahr-tuh
fixed-price menu	menú del migdia	muh-noo thuhl meech-dee-uh
wine list	la carta de vins	ah kahr-tuh thuh veens
glass of water	un got d'aigua	oon got dah-ee-gwah
glass of wine	una copa de vi	oo-nuh ko-pah thuh vee
bottle	una ampolla	oo-nuh am-pol-yuh
knife	un ganivet	oon gun-ee-veht
fork	una forquilla	oo-nuh foor-keel-yuh
spoon	una cullera	oo-nuh kool-yeh-ruh
breakfast	l'esmorzar	les-moor-sah
lunch	el dinar	uhl dee-nah
dinner	el sopar	uhl soo-pah
main course	el primer plat	uhl pree-meh plat
starters	els entrants	uhlz ehn-tranz
dish of the day	el plat del dia	uhl plat duhl dee-uh
coffee	el cafè	uhl kah-feh
rare	poc fet	pok fet
medium	al punt	ahl poon
well done	molt fet	mol fet

Menu Decoder

l'aigua mineral	lah-ee-gwuh mee-nuh-rahl	mineral water
sense gas/amb gas	sen-zuh gas/am gas	still sparkling
al forn	ahl forn	baked
l'all	lahlyuh	garlic
l'arròs	lahr-roz	rice
les botifarres	lahs boo-tee-fah-rahs	sausages

la carn	*lah karn*	meat
la ceba	*lah seh-buh*	onion
la cervesa	*lah-sehr-ve-sah*	beer
l'embotit	*lum-boo-teet*	cold meat
el filet	*uhl fee-let*	sirloin
el formatge	*uhl for-mah-djuh*	cheese
fregit	*freh-zheet*	fried
la fruita	*lah froo-ee-tah*	fruit
els fruits secs	*uhlz froo-eets seks*	nuts
les gambes	*lahs gam-bus*	prawns
el gelat	*uhl djuh-lat*	ice cream
la llagosta	*lah lyah-gos-tah*	lobster
la llet	*lah lyet*	milk
la llimona	*lah lyee-moh-nah*	lemon
la llimonada	*lah lyee-moh-nah-tuh*	lemonade
la mantega	*lah mahn-teh-gah*	butter
el marisc	*uhl muh-reesk*	seafood
la menestra	*lah muh-nehs-truh*	vegetable stew
l'oli	*loll-ee*	oil
les olives	*luhs oo-lee-vuhs*	olives
l'ou	*loh-oo*	egg
el pa	*uhl pah*	bread
el pastís	*uhl pahs-tees*	pie/cake
les patates	*lahs pah-tah-tuhs*	potatoes
el pebre	*uhl peh-bruh*	pepper
el peix	*uhl pehsh*	fish
el pernil salat serrà	*uhl puhr-neel suh-lat sehr-rah*	cured ham
el plàtan	*uhl plah-tun*	banana
el pollastre	*uhl poo-lyah-struh*	chicken
la poma	*la poh-mah*	apple
el porc	*uhl pohr*	pork
les postres	*lahs pohs-truhs*	dessert
rostit	*rohs-teet*	roast
la sal	*lah sahl*	salt
la salsa	*lah sahl-suh*	sauce
les salsitxes	*lahs sahl-see-chuhs*	sausages
sec	*sehk*	dry
la sopa	*lah soh-puh*	soup
el sucre	*uhl-soo-kruh*	sugar
la taronja	*lah tuh-rohn-djuh*	orange
el te	*uhl teh*	tea
les torrades	*lahs too-rah-thuhs*	toast
la vedella	*lah veh-theh-lyuh*	beef
el vi blanc	*uhl bee blang*	white wine
el vi negre	*uhl bee neh-gruh*	red wine
el vi rosat	*uhl bee roo-zaht*	rosé wine
el vinagre	*uhl bee-nah-gruh*	vinegar
el xai/el be	*uhl shahee/ uhl beh*	lamb
la xocolata	*lah shoo-koo-lah-tuh*	chocolate
el xoriç	*uhl shoo-rees*	red sausage

Numbers

0	zero	*seh-roo*
1	un (masc)	*oon*
	una (fem)	*oon-uh*
2	dos (masc)	*dohs*
	dues (fem)	*doo-uhs*
3	tres	*trehs*
4	quatre	*kwa-truh*
5	cinc	*seeng*
6	sis	*sees*
7	set	*set*
8	vuit	*voo-eet*
9	nou	*noh-oo*
10	deu	*deh-oo*
11	onze	*on-zuh*
12	dotze	*doh-dzuh*
13	tretze	*treh-dzuh*
14	catorze	*kah-tohr-dzuh*
15	quinze	*keen-zuh*
16	setze	*set-zuh*
17	disset	*dee-set*
18	divuit	*dee-voo-eet*
19	dinou	*dee-noh-oo*
20	vint	*been*
21	vint-i-un	*been-tee-oon*
22	vint-i-dos	*been-tee-dohs*
30	trenta	*tren-tah*
31	trenta-un	*tren-tah oon*
40	quaranta	*kwuh-ran-tah*
50	cinquanta	*seen-kwahn-tah*
60	seixanta	*seh-ee-shan-tah*
70	setanta	*seh-tan-tah*
80	vuitanta	*voo-ee-tan-tah*
90	noranta	*noh-ran-tah*
100	cent	*sen*
101	cent un	*sent oon*
102	cent dos	*sen dohs*
200	dos-cents	*dohs-sens*
	dues-centes (fem)	*doo-uhs sen-tuhs*
300	tres-cents	*trehs-senz*
400	quatre-cents	*kwah-truh-senz*
500	cinc-cents	*seeng-senz*
600	sis-cents	*sees-senz*
700	set-cents	*set-senz*
800	vuit-cents	*voo-eet-senz*
900	nou-cents	*noh-oo-cenz*
1,000	mil	*meel*
1,001	mil un	*meel oon*

Time

one minute	un minut	*oon mee-noot*
one hour	una hora	*oo-nuh oh-ruh*
half an hour	mitja hora	*mee-juh oh-ruh*
Monday	dilluns	*dee-lyoonz*
Tuesday	dimarts	*dee-marts*
Wednesday	dimecres	*dee-meh-kruhs*
Thursday	dijous	*dee-zhoh-oos*
Friday	divendres	*dee-ven-druhs*
Saturday	dissabte	*dee-sab-tuh*
Sunday	diumenge	*dee-oo-men-juh*